SOCCER

HUMOR

By

Charles Hellman and Robert Tiritilli

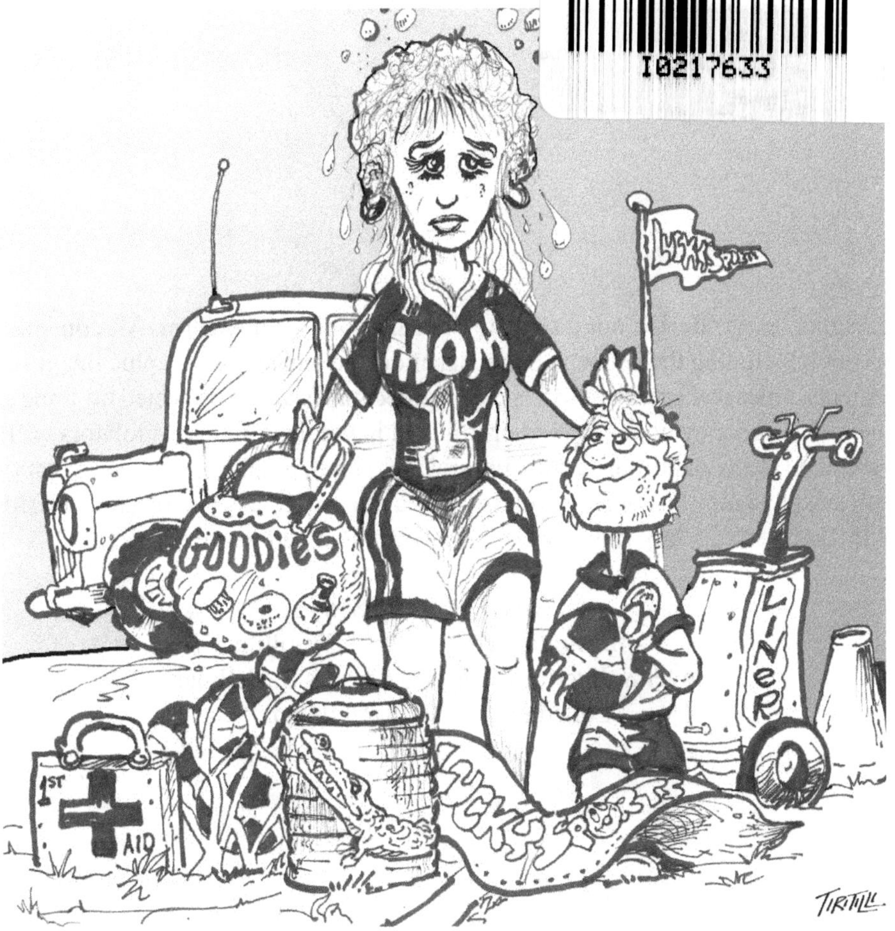
MOM
1
GOODIES
1ST
AID
LINER
TIRITILLI

Copyright 2019

ALL RIGHT RESERVED
78218 Silverleaf Crt.
Palm Desert, CA 92211
www.LuckySportsHumor.com

All rights reserved. Do not duplicate or redistribute in any form. All contents of this book including the concept, elements of design and layout, graphic images and elements, unless otherwise noted, is copyrighted material and protected by trade and other laws and may not be copied or imitated in whole or in part. Violators will be prosecuted to the maximum extent possible. No logo, graphic, character or caption from any page may be copied or retransmitted unless expressly permitted in writing by LuckySports$_{TM}$. Any rights not expressly granted herein are reserved.

ISBN 9780935938364
Illustrations by Robert A. Tiritilli
Cover & Interior Design by Charles S. Hellman
Edited by Charles S. Hellman

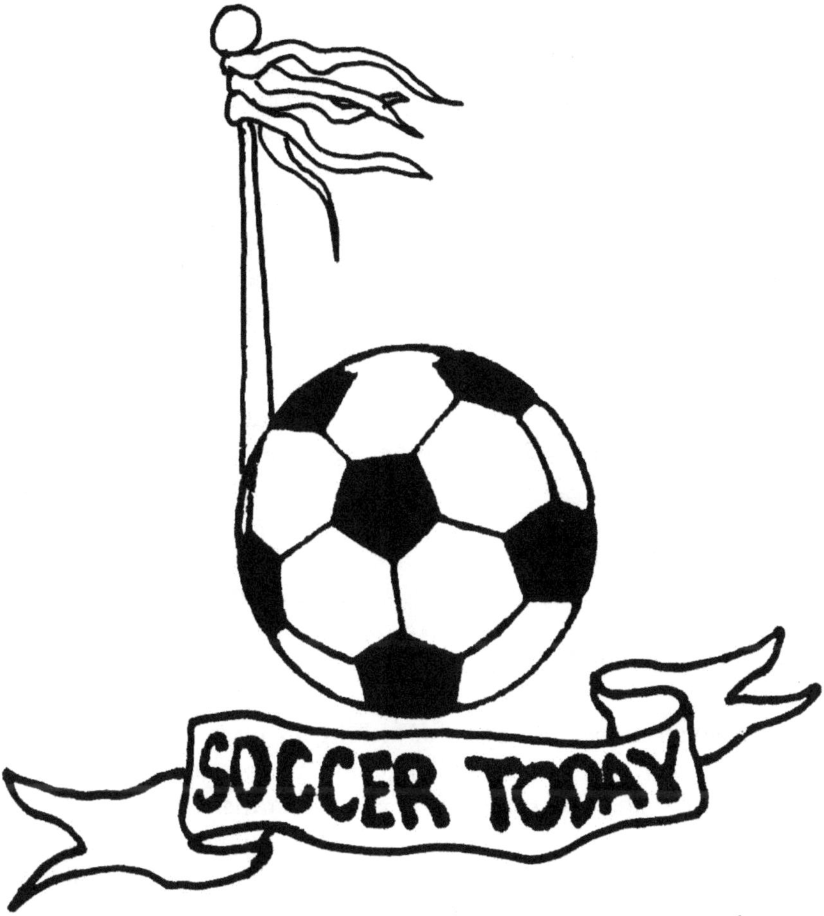
SOCCER TODAY
TIRITILLI

Soccer Review

There is a point in the life of every novice and aficionado soccer fan when cartoons based on wordplay and images that are hysterically funny. This soccer humor book is for those who are at that joyous stage in life.

The sport of soccer (called fútbol in most of the world) is the world's most popular sport. In soccer there are two teams of eleven players. Soccer is played on a large grass field with a goal at each end. The object of the game is to get the soccer ball into the opposing team's goal. Perhaps no sport has more words, terms and phrases that lend themselves to humorous reinterpretation based on their literal meaning than soccer

Charles S. Hellman and Robert A. Tiritilli have clearly kept their ability to look at the world through ingenuous eyes, and we are the beneficiaries of their vision. You will feel many years younger as you recall the last time you saw the humor in "grownups" taking a sport too seriously.

The book contains over 100 one-paneled, pen and ink drawings that are reproduced in black and white except on the front and back cover of this soft cover book.

The front cover captures one of the better cartoons and gives you a sense of this book at its best ... when it shifts the meaning of a soccer phrase into another one ... but still within a soccer context. Play on words or images gives humor double meaning. The double whammy effect.

Soccer has evolved from the sport of kicking a rudimentary animal-hide ball around into the World Cup sport it is today. Records trace the history of soccer back more than 2,000 years ago to ancient China.

These cartoons will tickle your funny bone. Novices, however, will have a few of the cartoons explained to them (as employing soccer terms) they may not know a yellow card from a credit card.

If you are knowledgeable to figure out the "Liverpool" cartoons without explanation, this book could be a good gift.

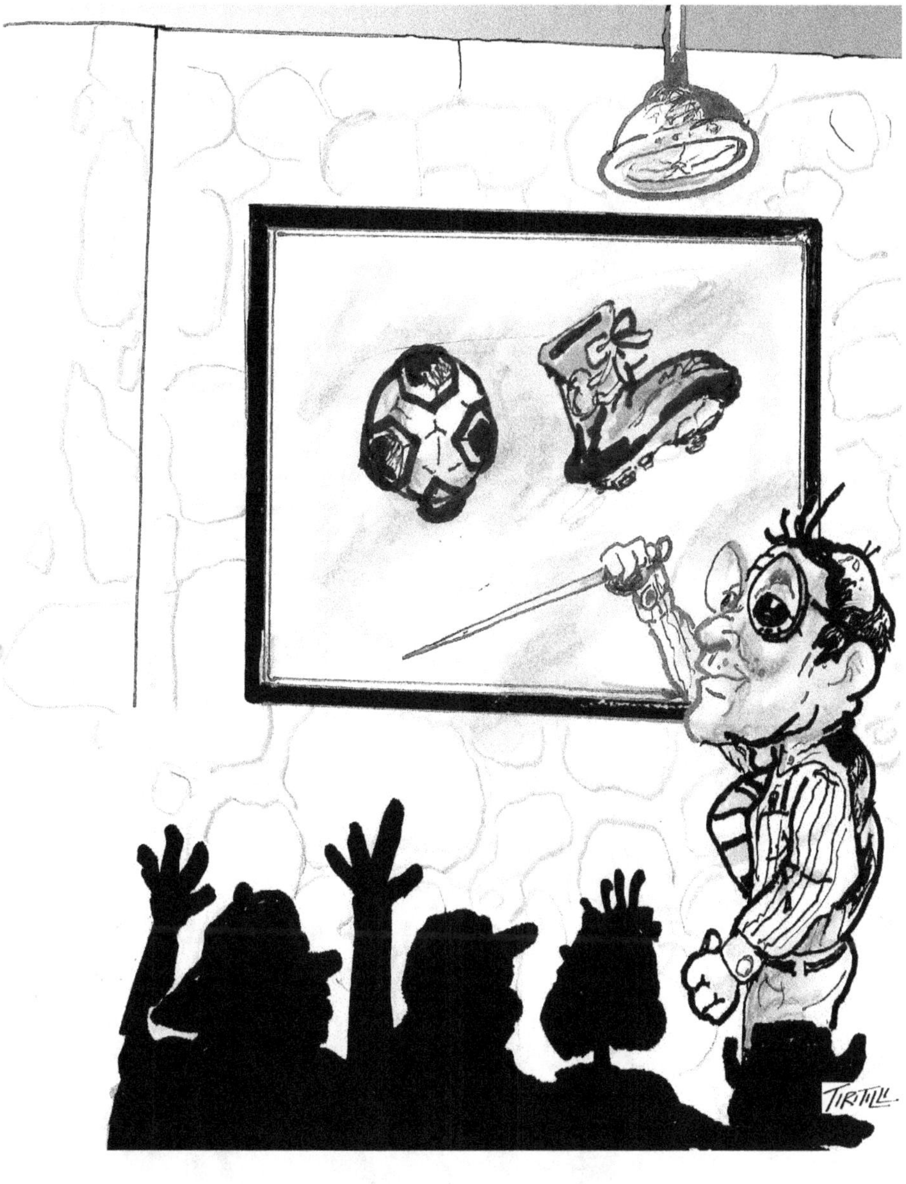
TIRITILLI

Soccer 101

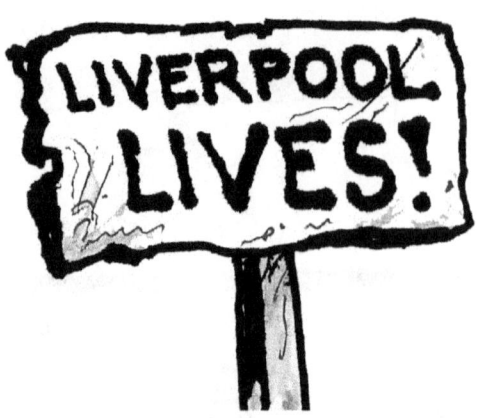

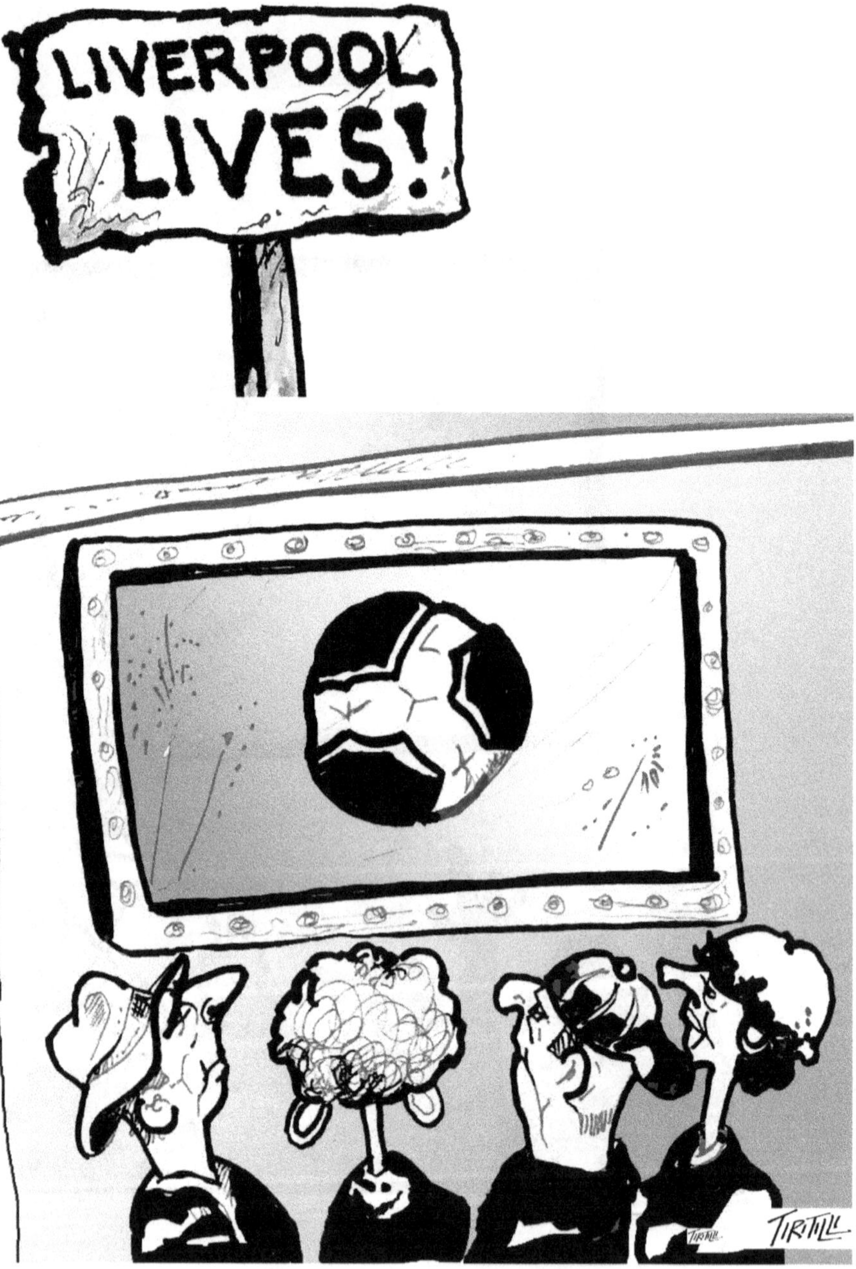
LIVERPOOL
LIVES!

"It's a new planet called SOCCER!"

"Soccer meditation, my ass!"

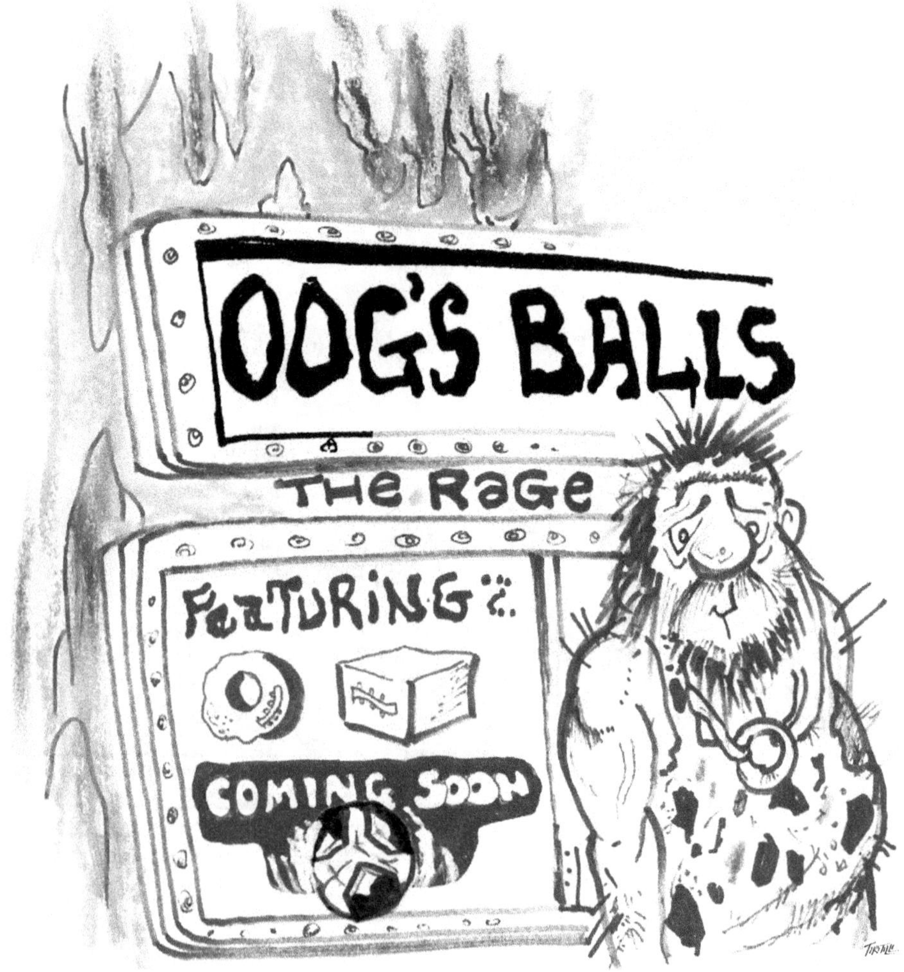
OOG'S BALLS
THE RAGE
FEATURING:
COMING SOON

Soccer Mom

"Which one of you clowns played soccer with Péle?"

Mythical Match - Loch Ness Monster vs Puff the Magic Dragon

He was diagnosed as having a bad case of soccer cleats

"Don't worry, its not contagious!"

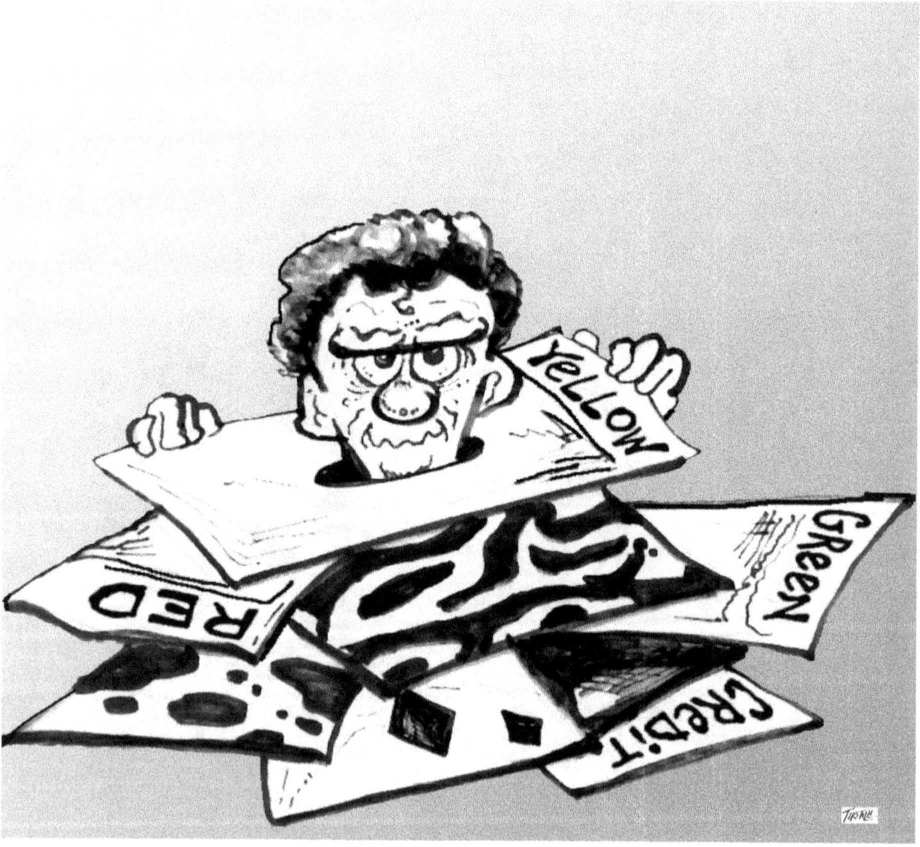
YeLLOW
GReeN
RED
CReDiT

Pick a card

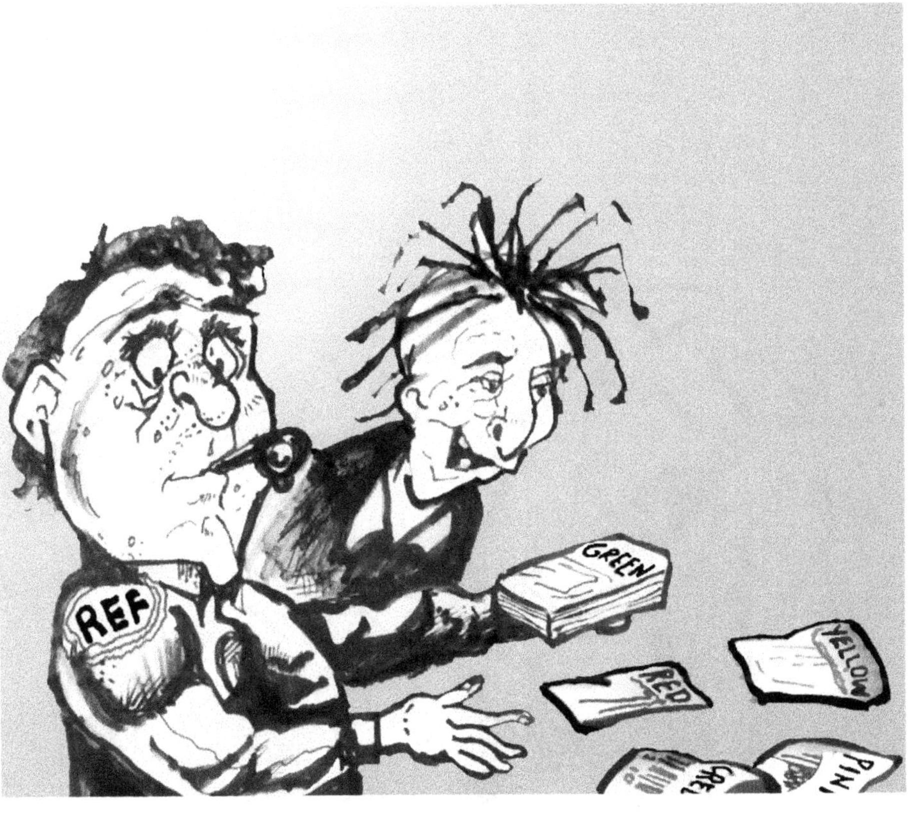
REF
GREEN
RED
YELLOW

"Wanna play 52 card pick-up?"

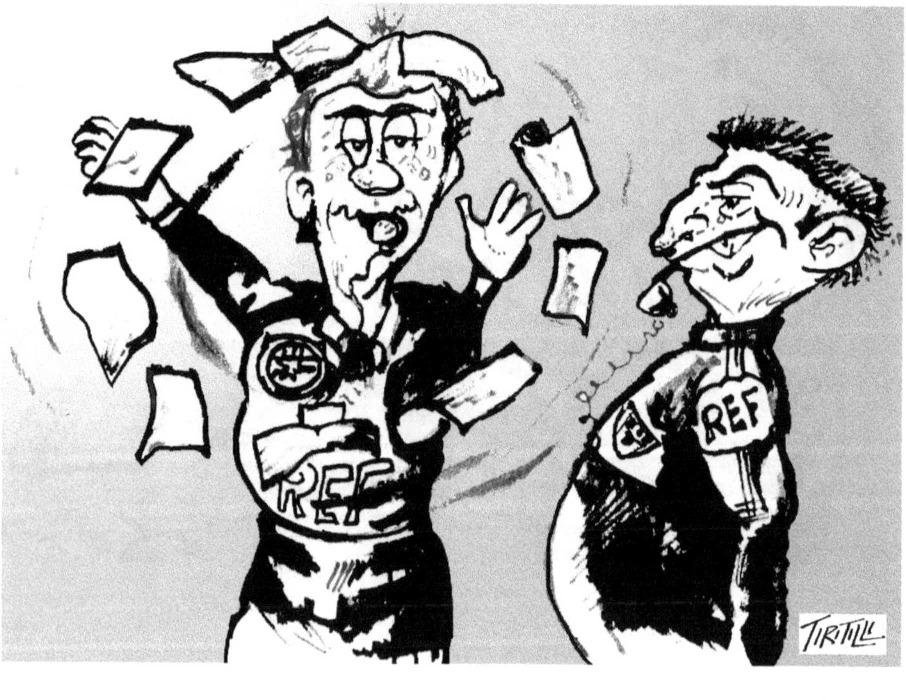
REF
REF
TIRITILLI

Card Trick

Sold Drugs to soccer kids

Wonderdini's silly soccer trick!

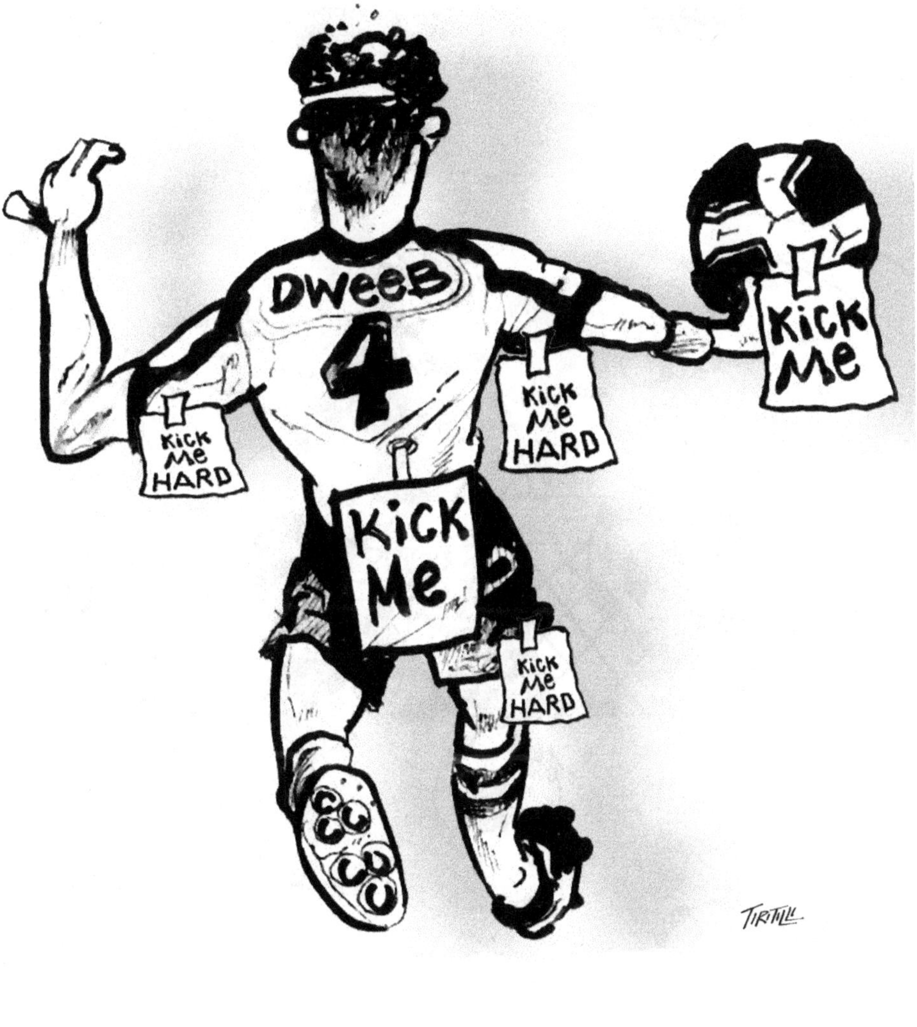
DWEEB
4
KICK ME HARD
KICK ME HARD
KICK ME
KICK ME
KICK ME HARD
TIRITILLI

Practical jokes

Experimental Soccer Ball Patch

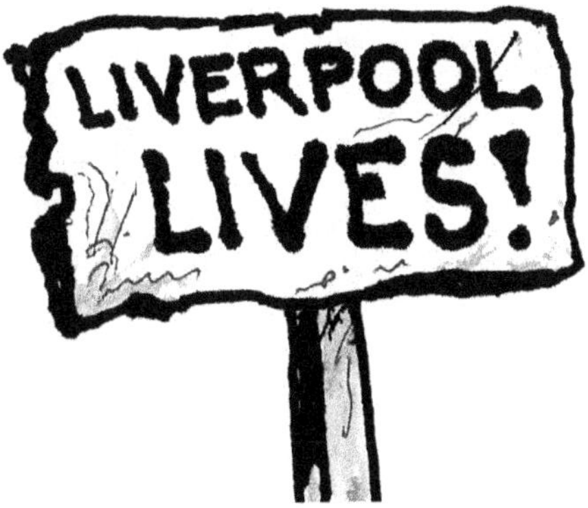
LIVERPOOL
LIVES!

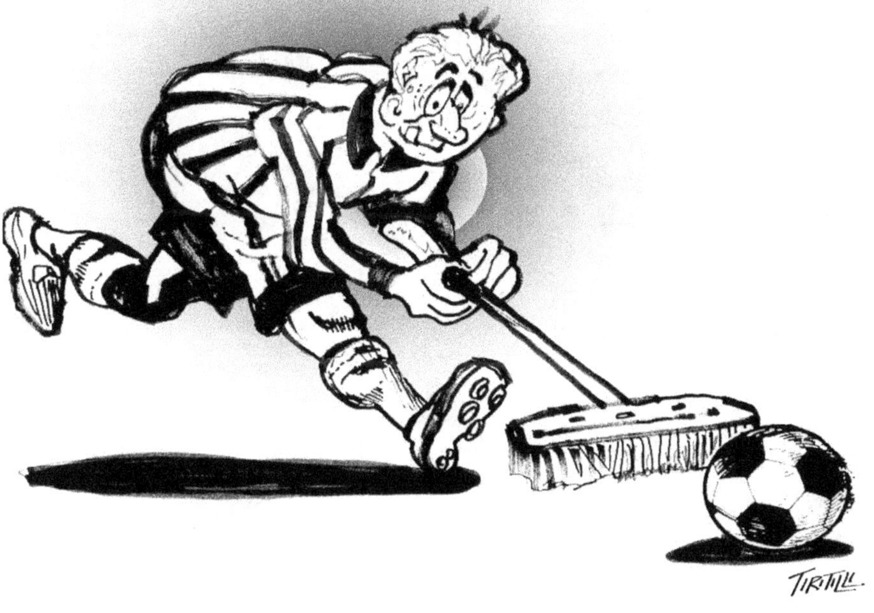

Sweeper

"Too bad he has two left feet!"

Professor Putz tries to prove soccer is the most played sport in the world

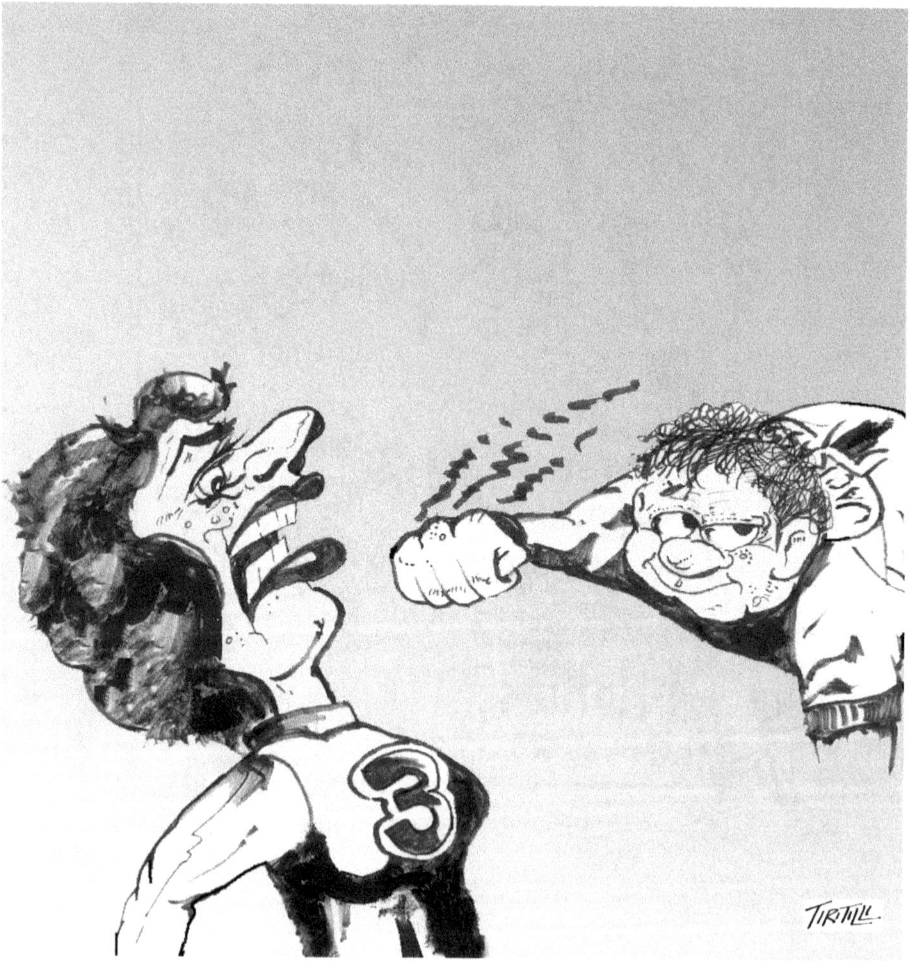
TIRITILLI

Sock-Her

Scissors kick

Senior soccer player wants *real* medical help!

Millennials Games Finals!

Review officals make mistake --- replay Normandy Invasion

"This game & reality leave a lot to the imagination."

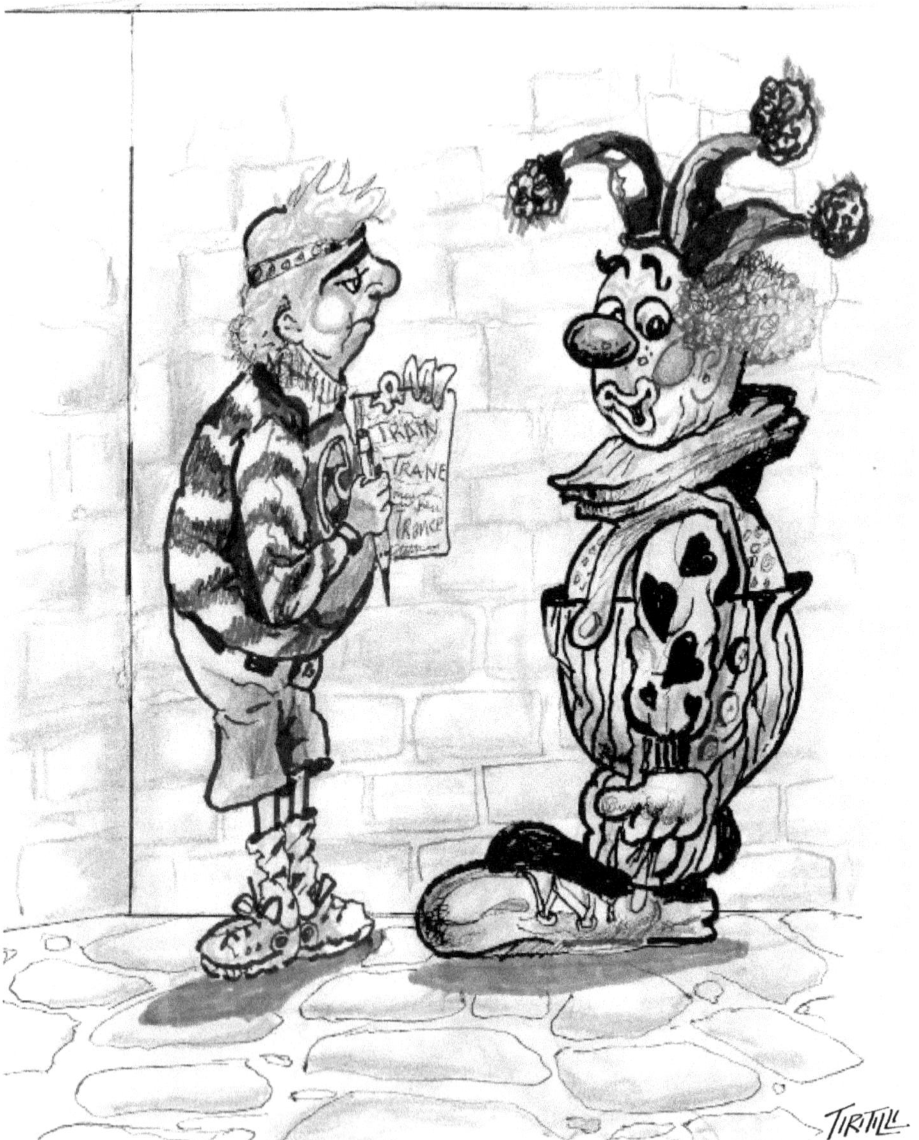
TRAIN
TRANE
TRANCE
TIRITILLI

"You want to befriend me?"

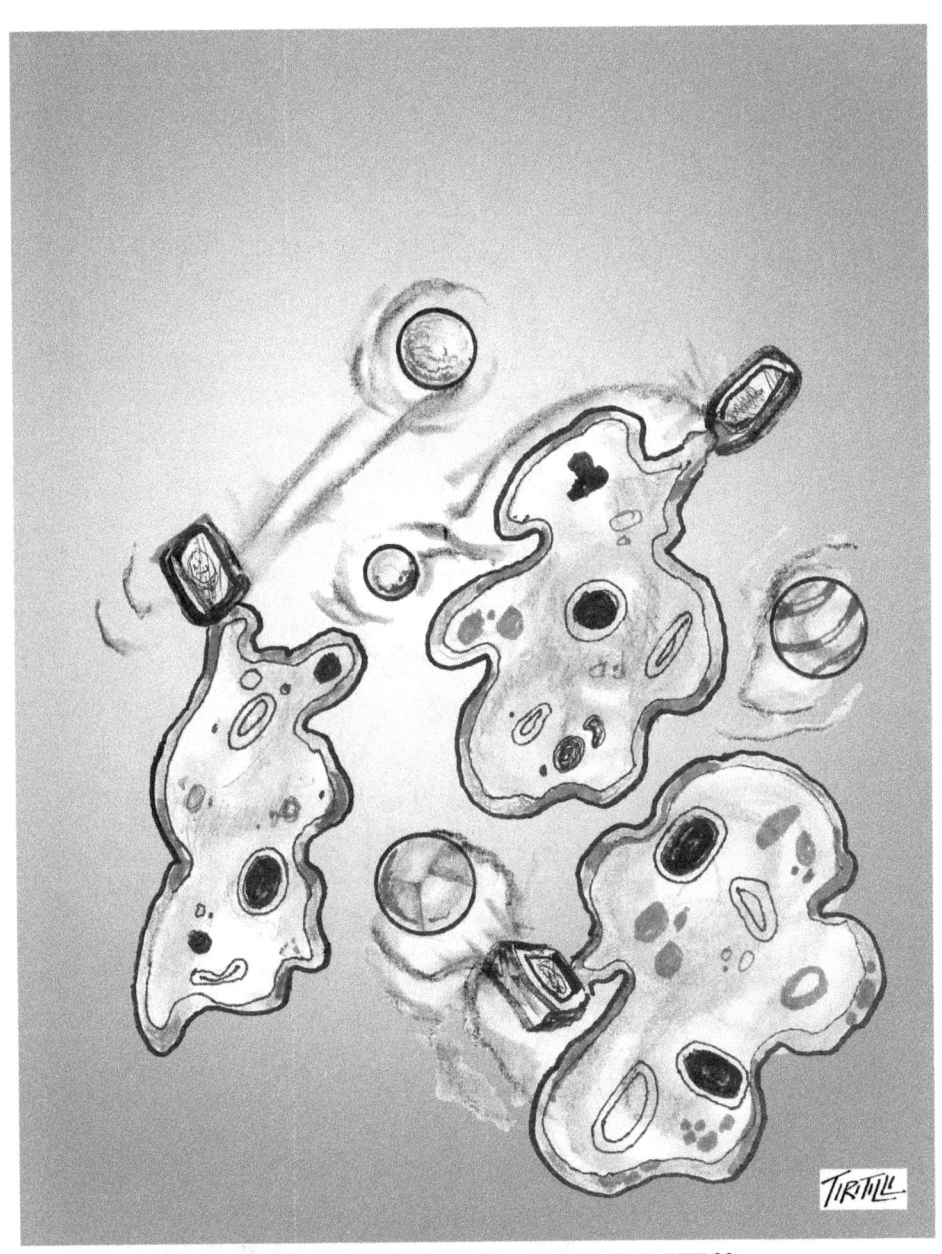

Red & white "CELL PHONE" games

"Who received a RED card last week?"

"Who wants to represent
Team Management and Spirit."

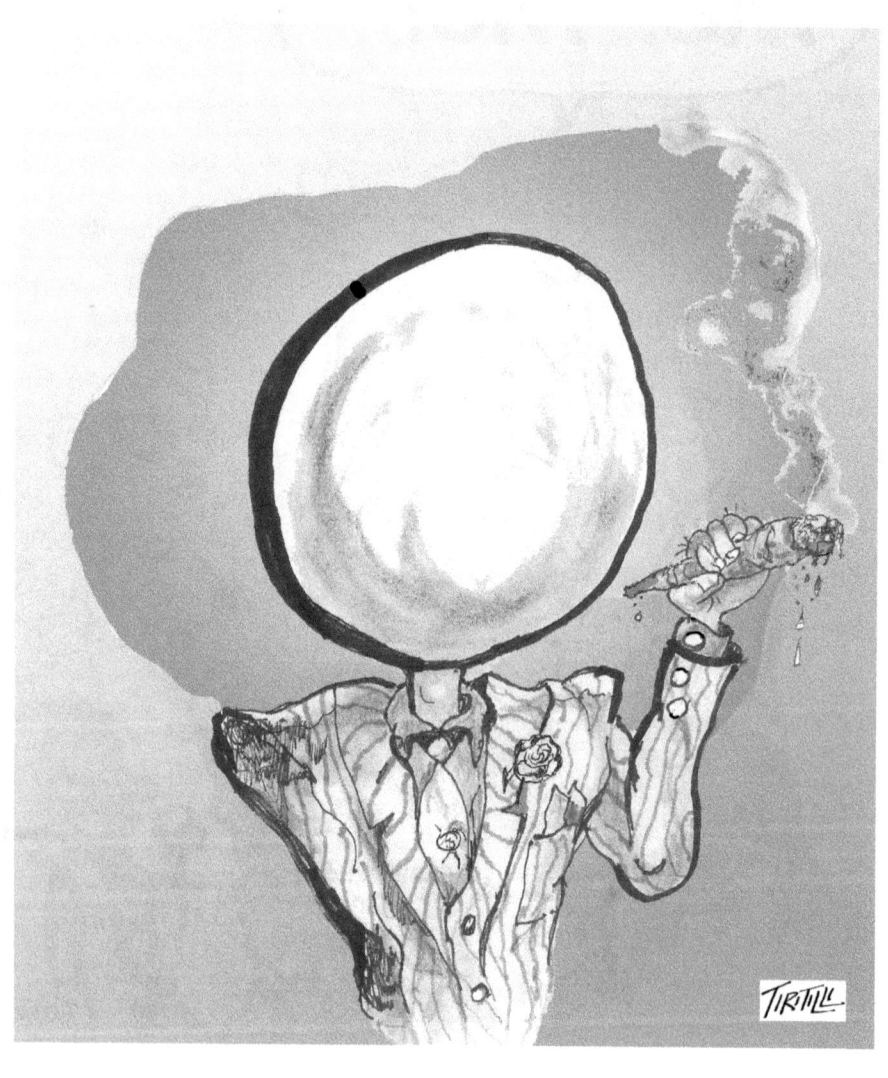

The face of soccer without panels

"So you think you're ready to play against Liverpool, huh?

"Her first soccer contract"

"Who should I befriend,
if your team wins?"

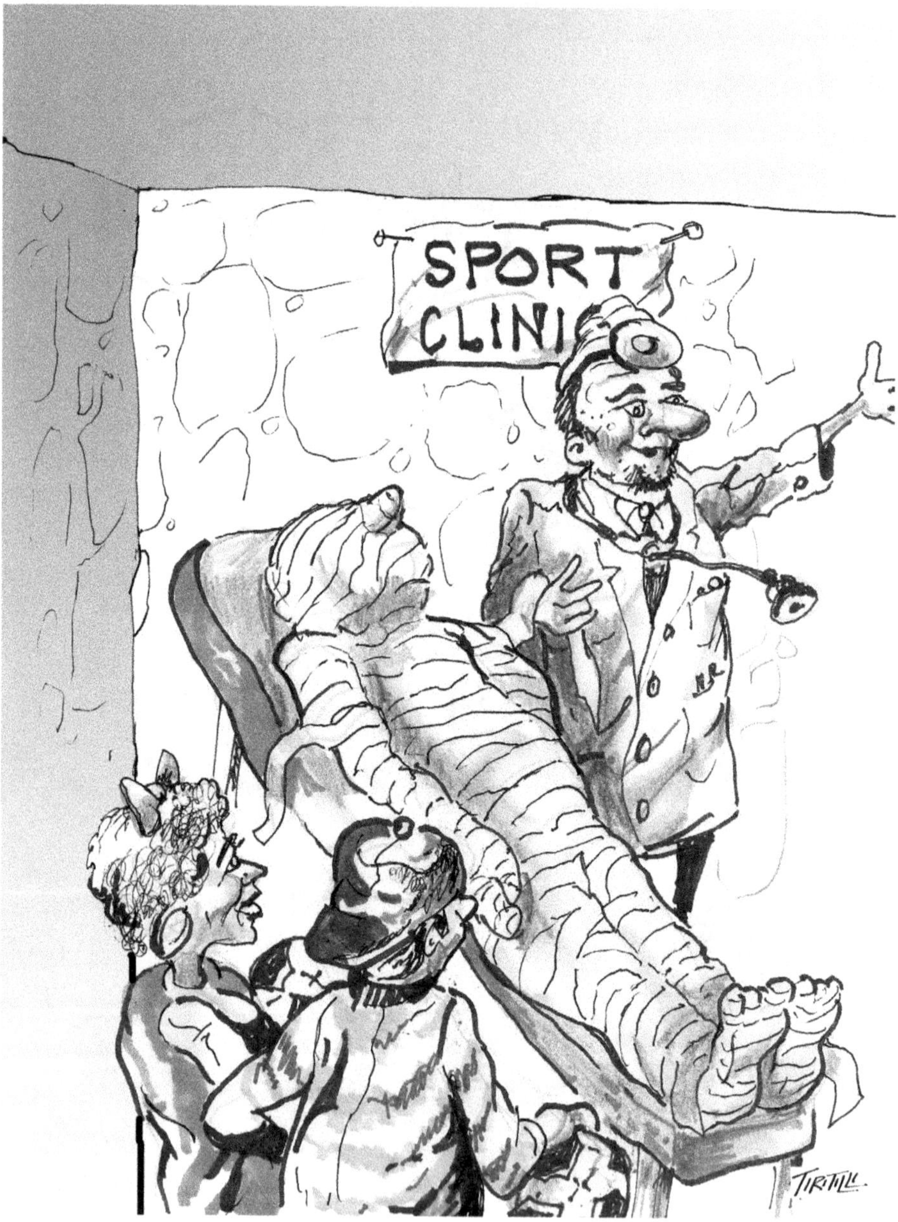
SPORT
CLINI

"It's a wrap!"

"Look Mom! We played the whole game and they forgot to keep score.

"Listen... I transferred our IRA and 401K to the soccer pool.

"Hey Soccer mascots, Kemosabee wants to see your papers before entering."

"My team fired me for an egg.
They said the egg came first!"

Finger pointing at the Sports' Negotiation Committee Meeting

"According to my calculations, Liverpool will beat Manchester United.

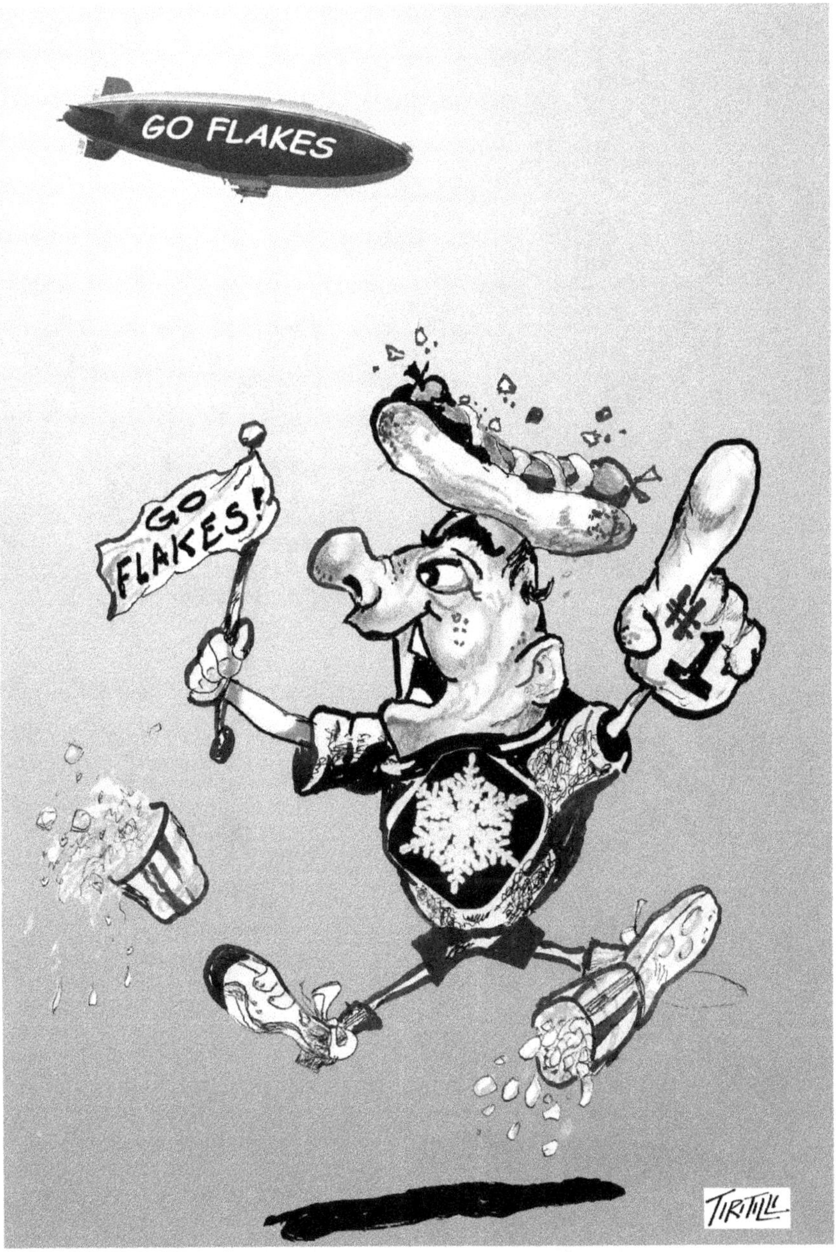
GO FLAKES
GO FLAKES!
#1
TIRITILLI

Soccer fan

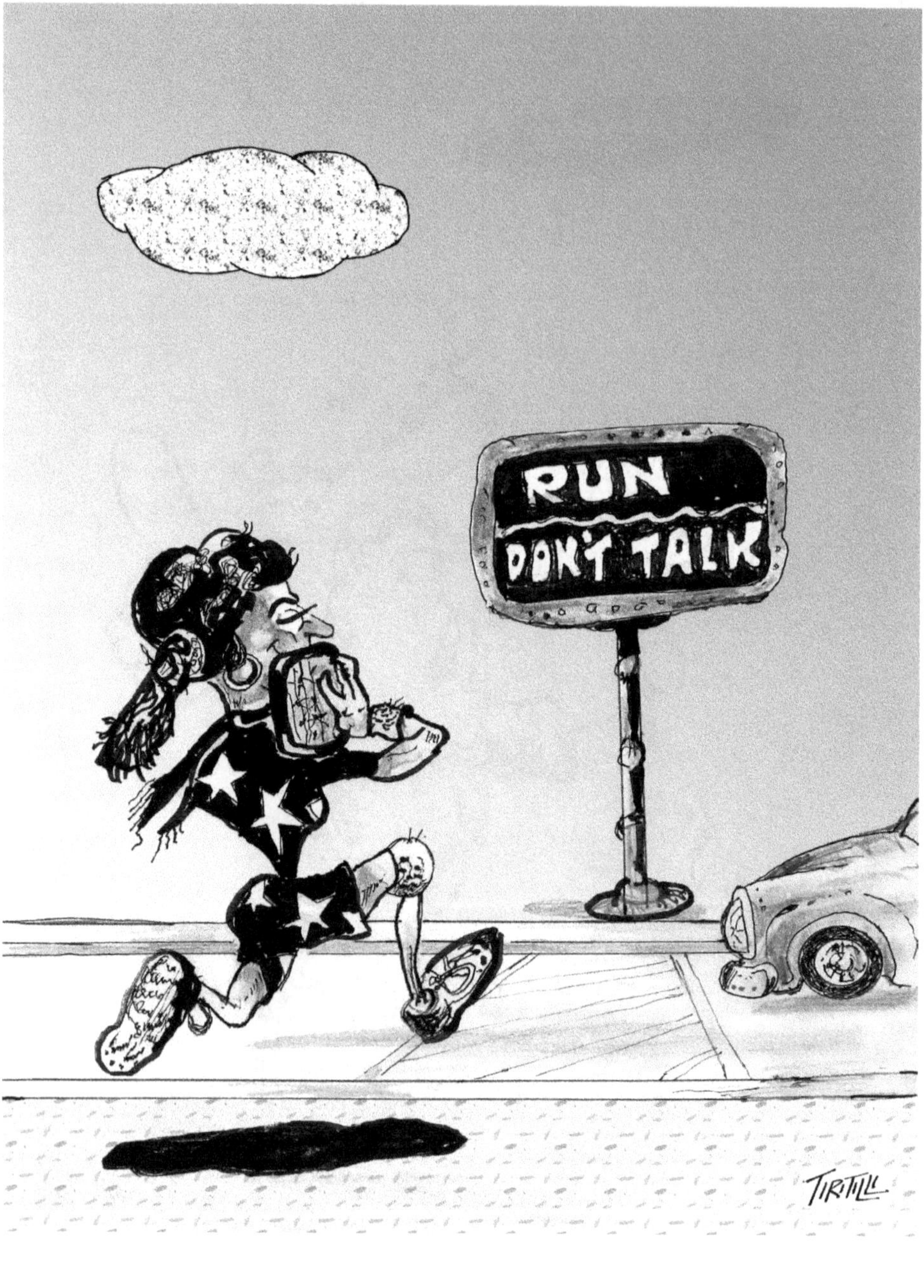
RUN
DON'T TALK

"OK, we'll get a soccer training video starring you!"

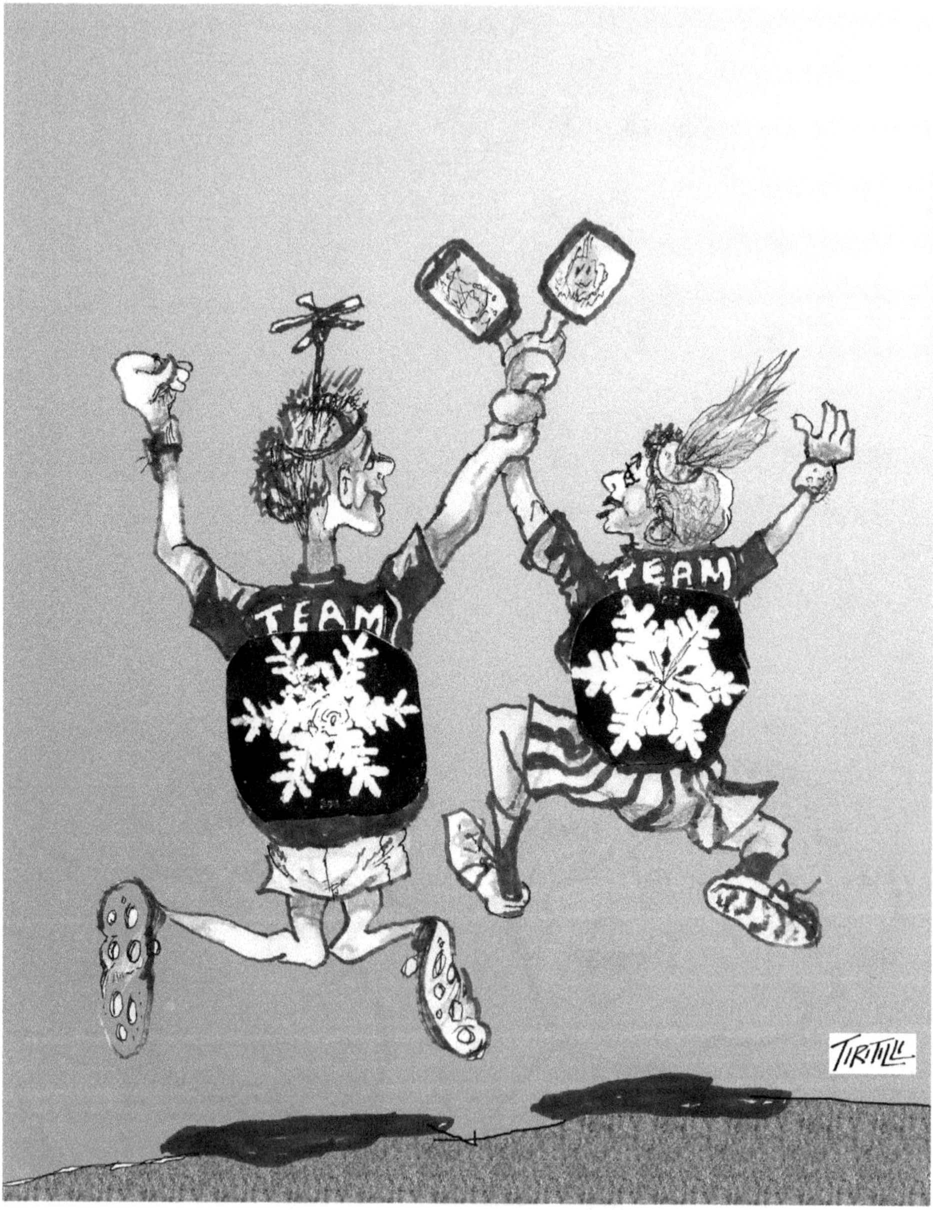
TEAM
TEAM
TIRITILLI

Millennials, call 911!

"Look Mom!
Look what I got for signing-up!"

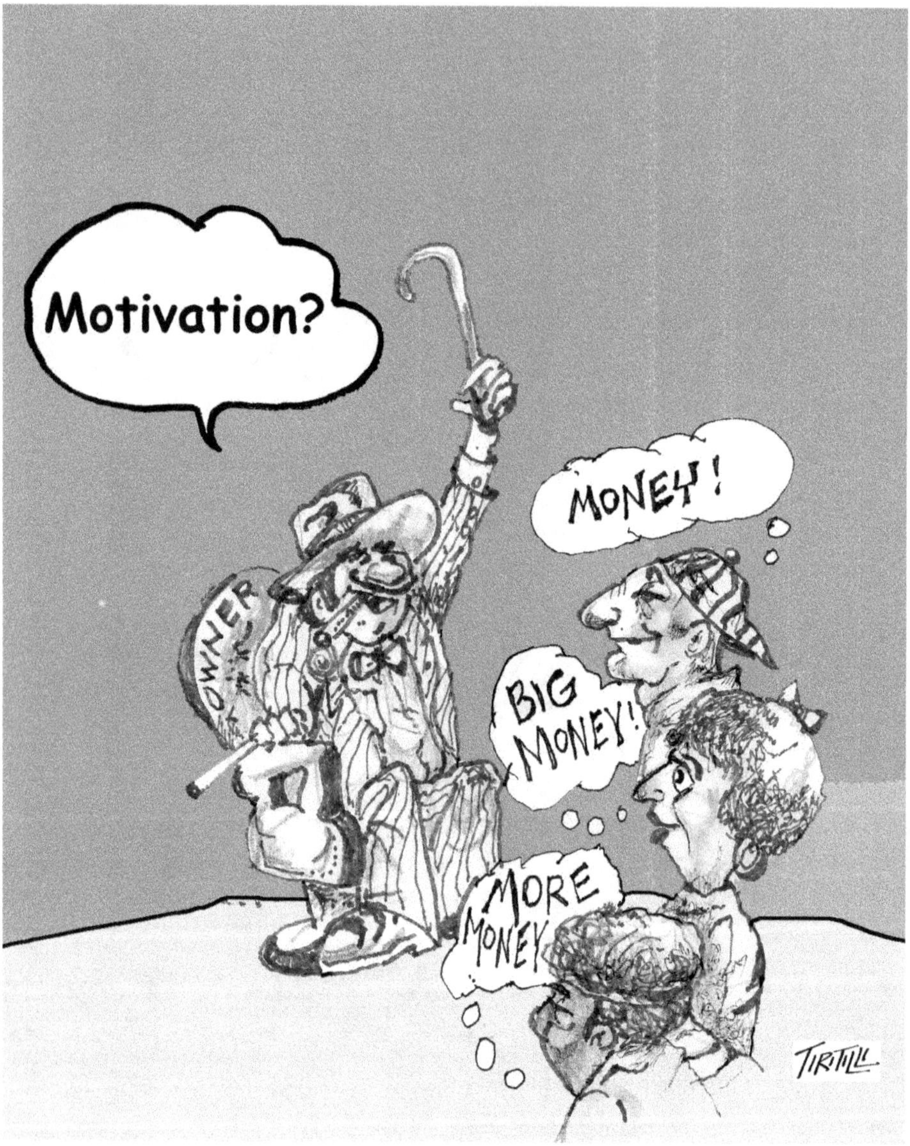
Motivation?
OWNER
MONEY!
BIG MONEY!
MORE MONEY
TIRITILLI

"OK, what motives us?"

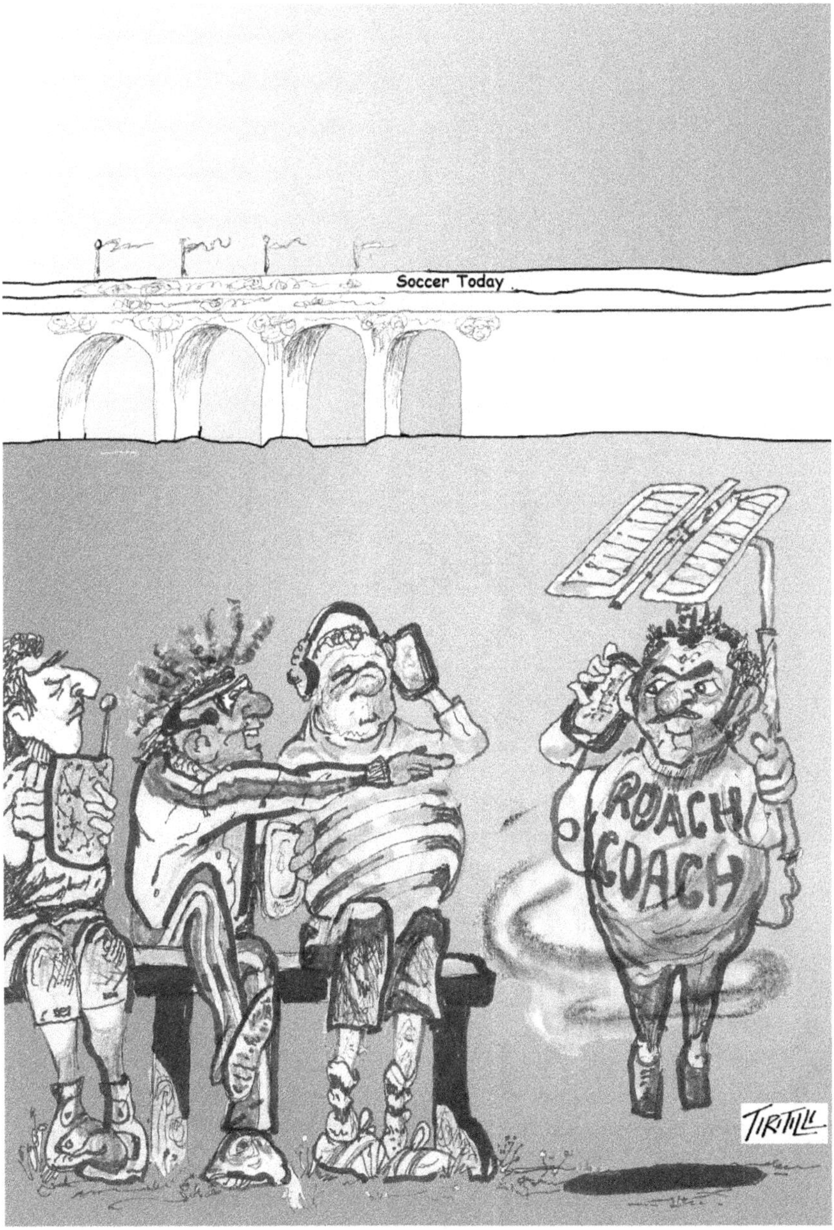
Soccer Today
ROACH COACH
TIRITILLI

“He’s got WiFi!”

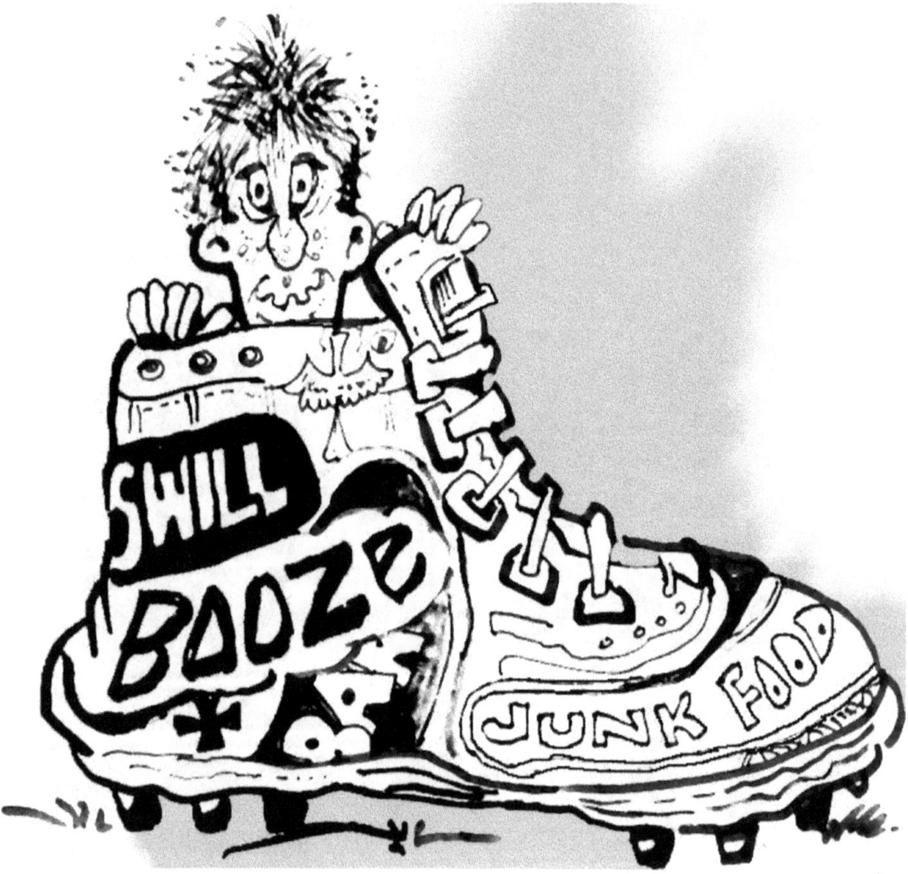
SWILL
BOOZE
JUNK FOOD

Big Shoe Contract

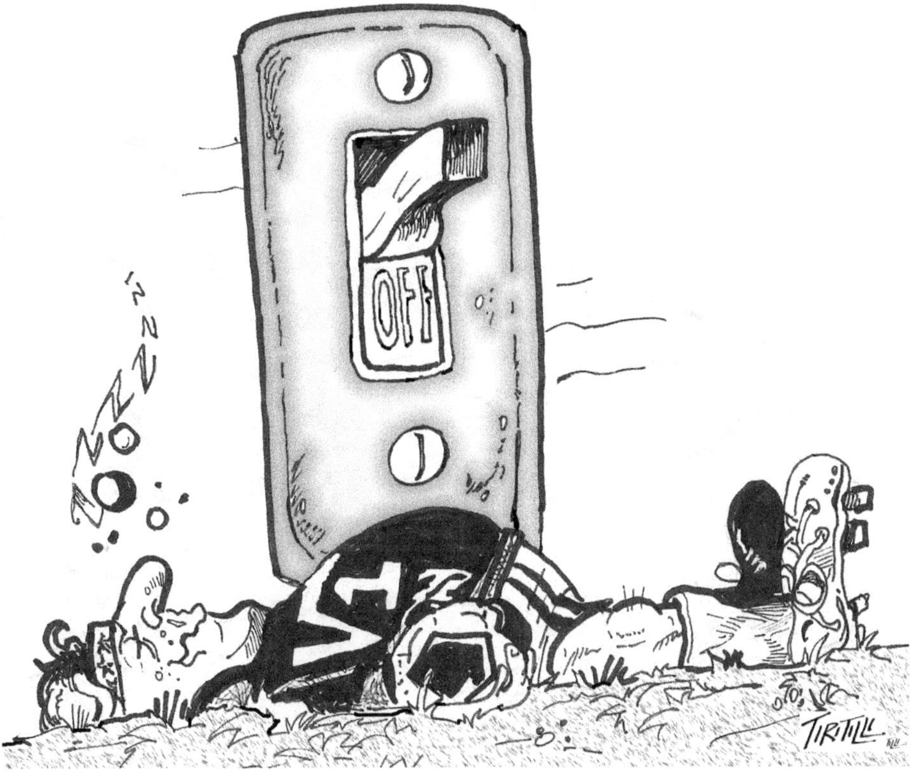
OFF

Asleep at the switch

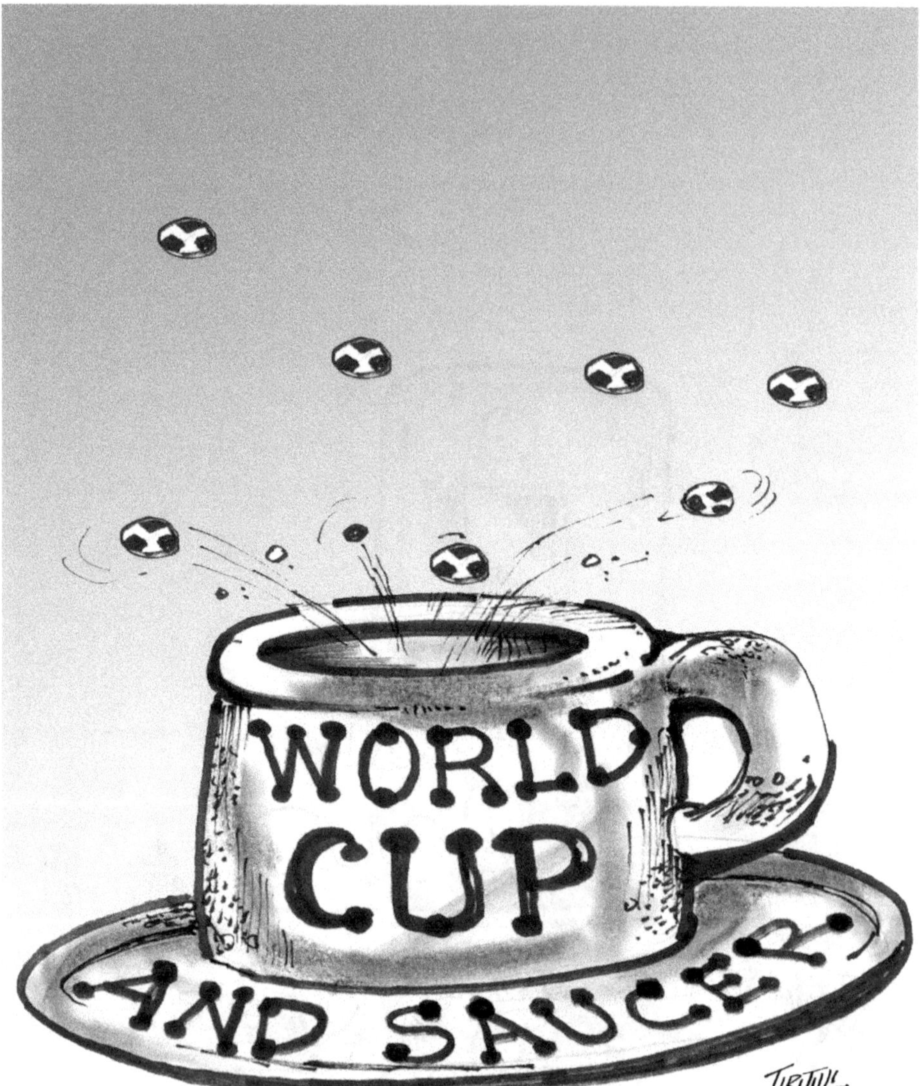
WORLD
CUP
AND SAUCER
TIRITILLI

Referee Flatfoot gets an early start as a whistleblower on his 4th birthday.

**"You're so slow,
your shadow refuses to follow you!"**

"He must be a soccer player!"

This ball suffers from over aerobics.

"I've got to let you go.
You have a winning disorder."

"Of course, your team still loves you, we are too tired to hate you!"

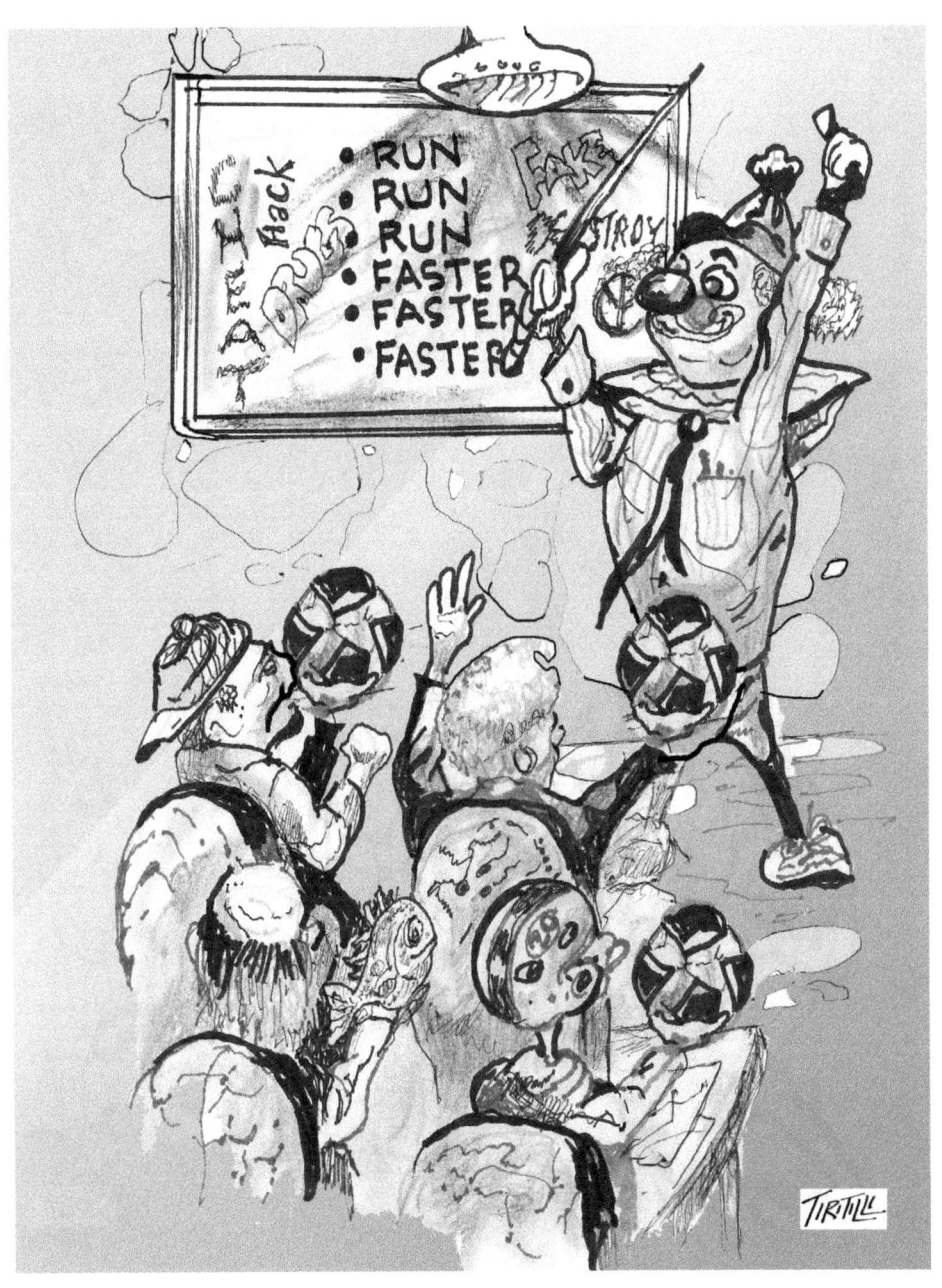

"Who wants tickets for the Liverpool - Manchester United game?"

He's not ancient had they measured his life expectancy with an hour glass.

Even his eye lashes are out of shape.

Alfonso's brain storm turns into a nuclear event

"How long have you been a couch potato?"

"Honesty is always the best policy... unfortuately it's definity not ours!"

Ultimate Soccer Stadium fan uniform

Alexander Graham Bell invents the "CELL PHONE" --- becomes 1st sports telemarker!

"Use Twitter or be a sportwit!"

"Oh how I miss those old sportswriter briefings."

"Did you know I once rode with Péle."

"I use to be a star soccer player, but now I am just a waterboy."

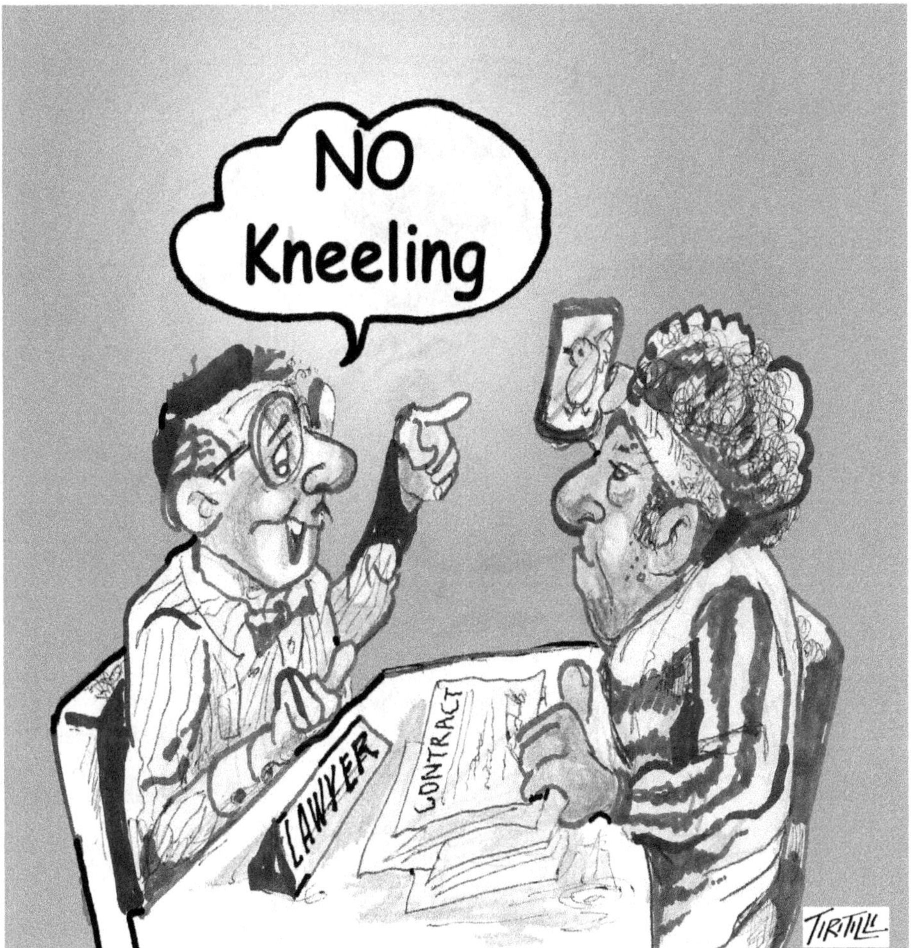
NO Kneeling
LAWYER
CONTRACT
TIRITILLI

"I don't know why the chicken crossed the road, do you?"

"I changed my soccer facebook account password to 123 kick!"

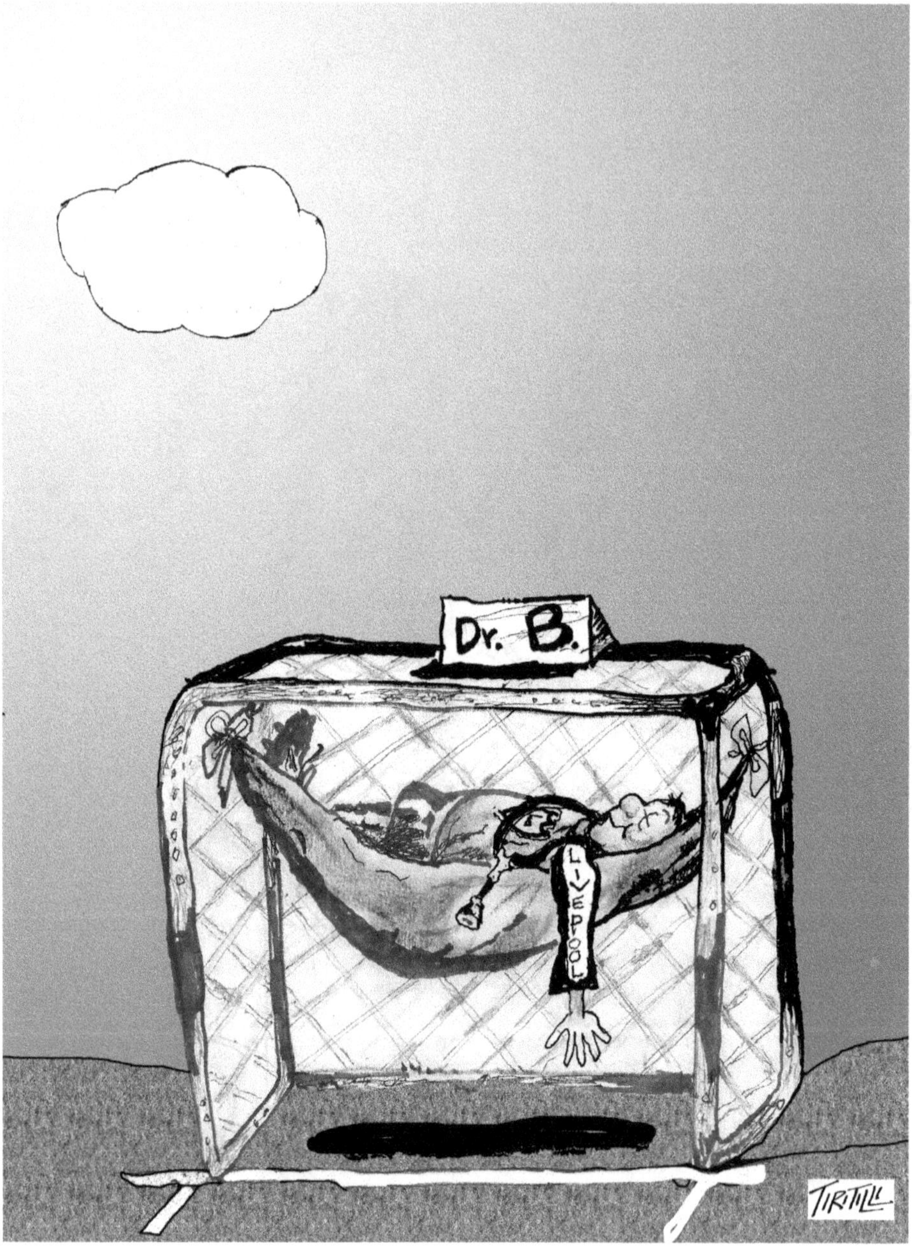
Dr. B.
LIVEPOOL
TIRITILLI

Relaxing

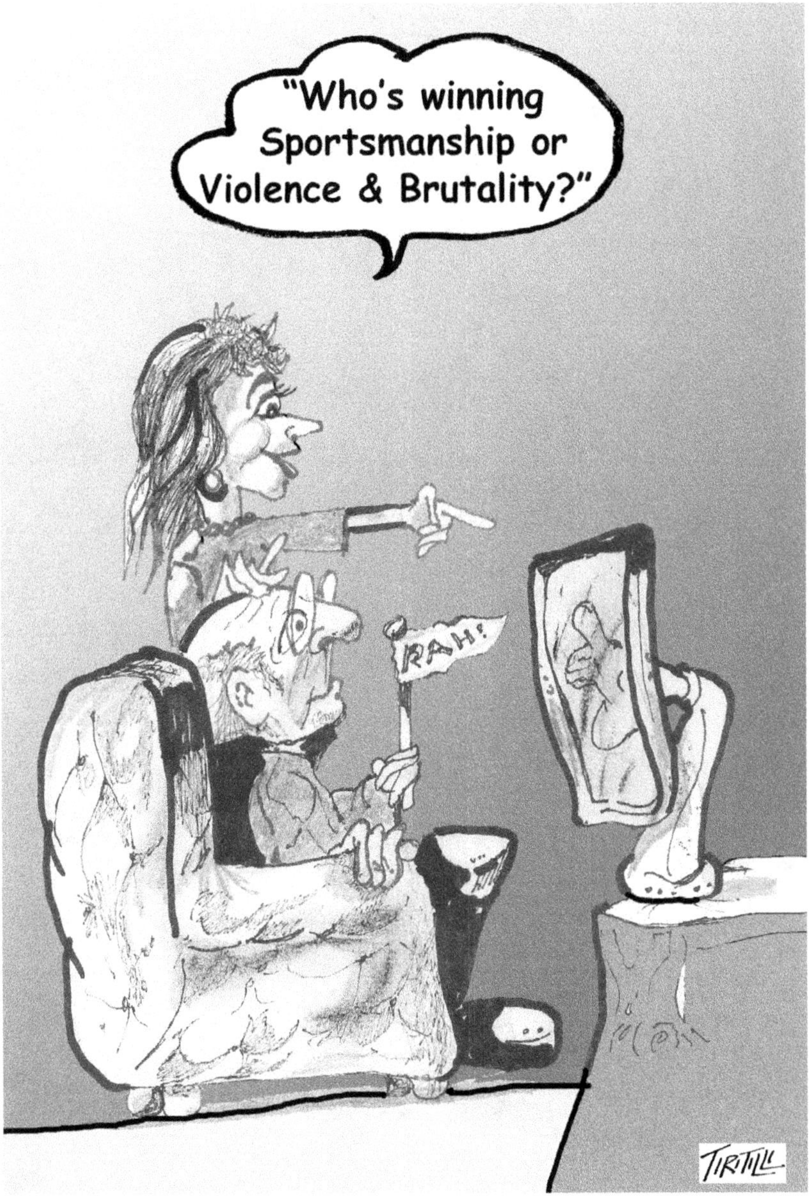
"Who's winning Sportsmanship or Violence & Brutality?"
RAH!
TIRITILLI

"Sorry, I didn't play for Liverpool."

Dr. Malet invents the sport concussion... brings problem to a head!

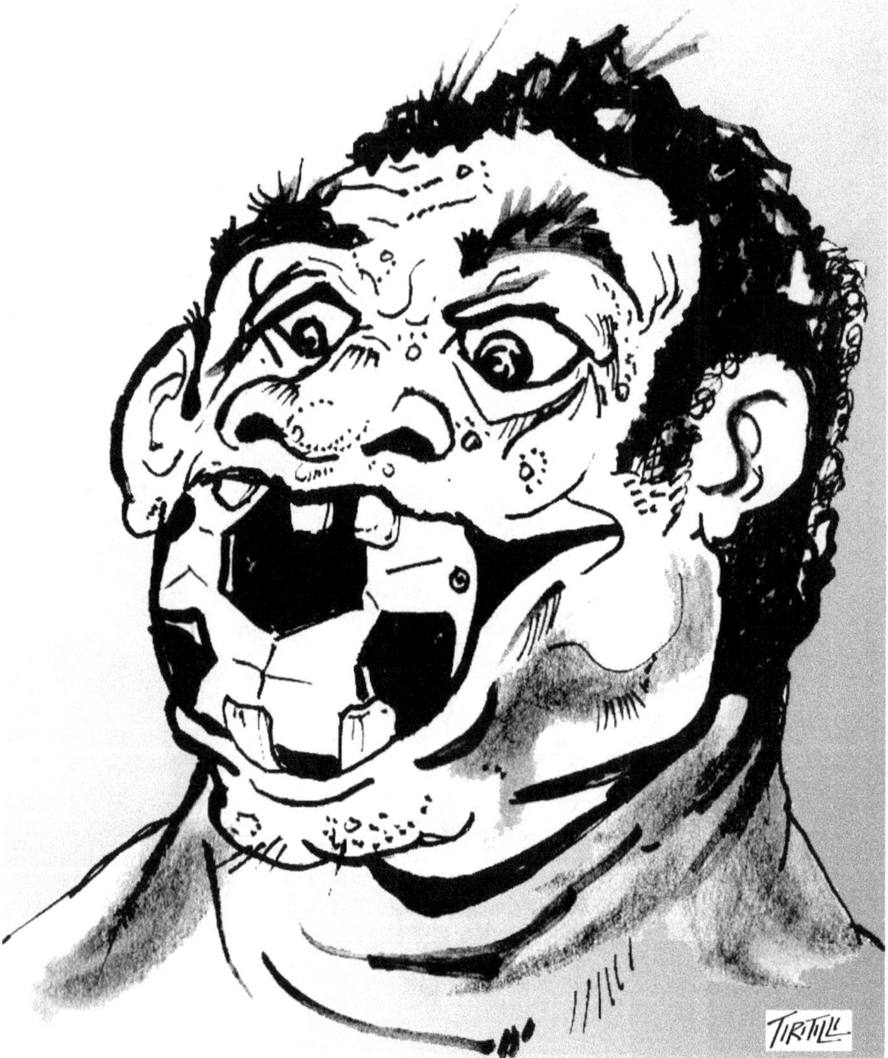

"It tastes like chicken!"

"Never go through life without GOALS!"

"It's just a precautionary procedure."

"Those last 3 soccer wins where due to the coach wearing his LUCKY SOCKS!"

"This is a soccer ball.
If you want a 2nd opinion, go ahead."

The doctor assured him that he is not going to feel a thing.

"You don't have MAD COW disease; you have SOCCER FRENZY."

First soccer game; first injury

Cumma amma wanna finds early soccer ball --- Goes on a roll!

"Maybe *less* exercise will help!"

"Does my butt look too BIG?"

Millennial soccer pilates

"Professor...
did Liverpool have a team then?"

Red card...
unnecessary roughness.

Proessor Fritz discovers the Soccer Ball Burial Grounds

"Of course, we want you on the team!"

Their goal is starting to look like a zoo!

Ultimate left winger

LOOK OUT...
The dreaded Midfield Cross

Sigfried kicks the Golden Goal

FIFA invents the Penalty Box

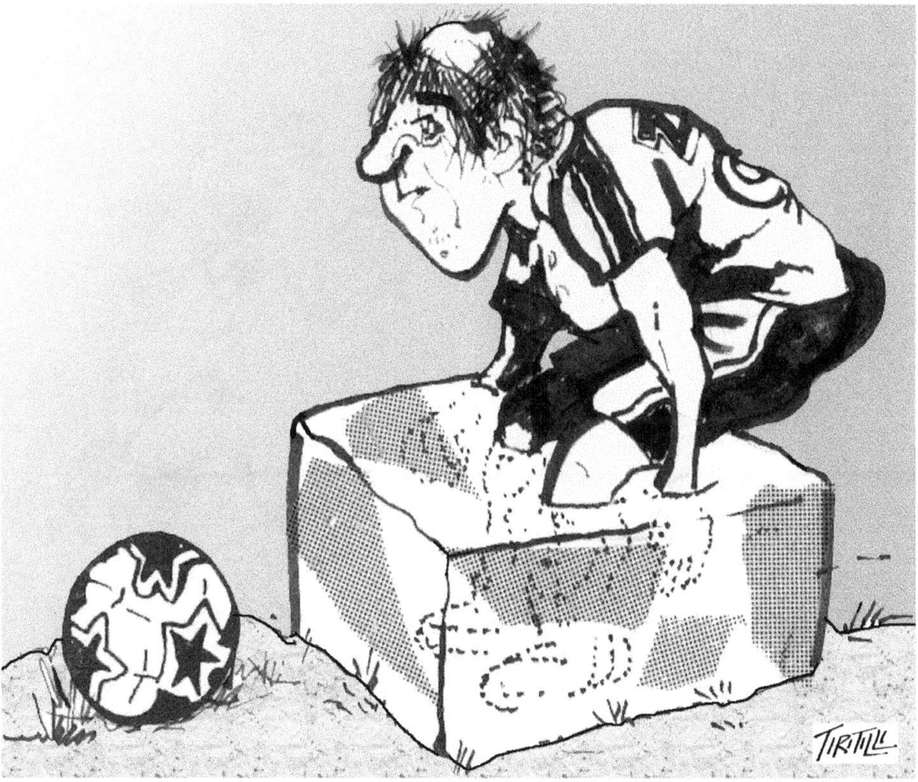
TIRITILLI

ICED!

"We don't cheat...
but we never play fair!"

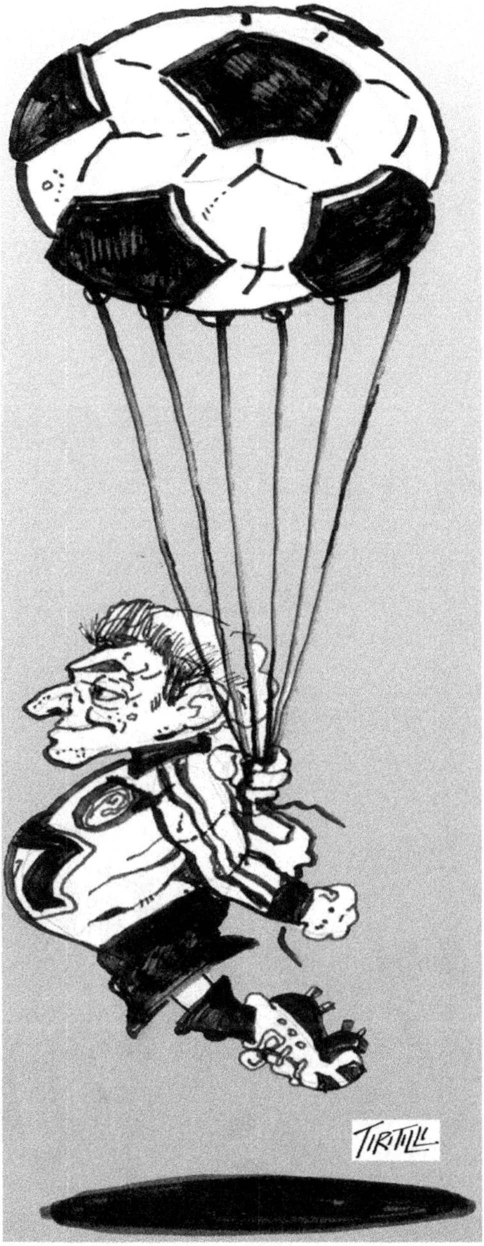
TIRITILLI

High Flyer

**Natives find Amelia Earhart...
"All Jungle" World Cup.**

World Cup Team Germany launches all out arerial attack

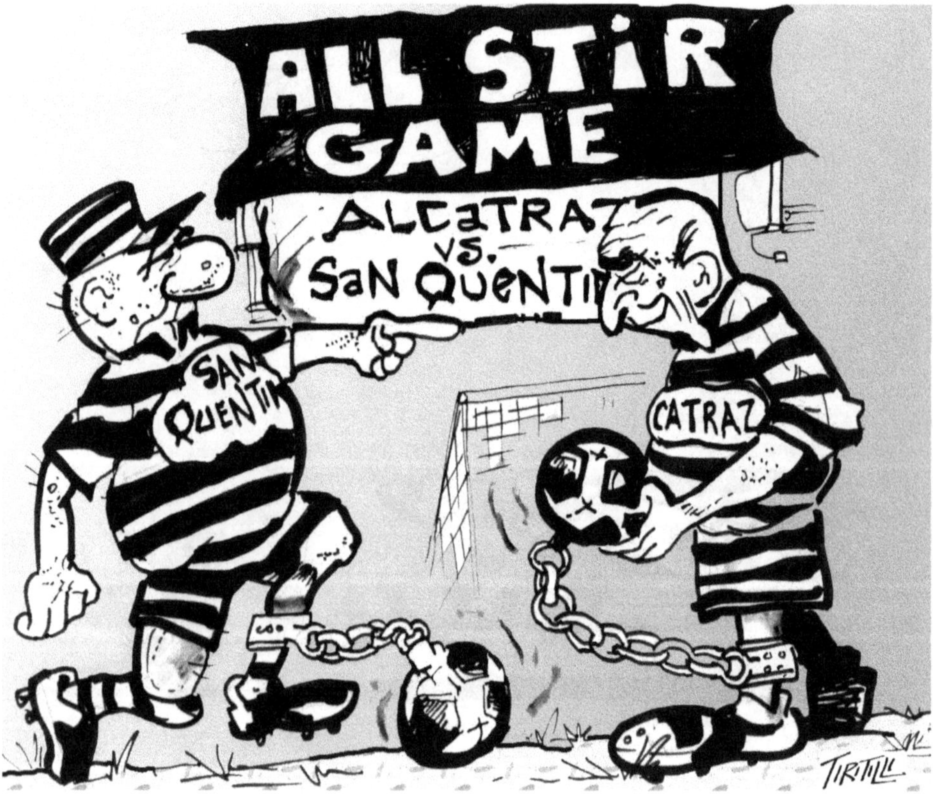
ALL STIR GAME
ALCATRAZ
VS.
SAN QUENTI
SAN QUENTI
CATRAZ
TIRITILLI

"I heard from an earthing that they play a version of our soccer!"

"Relax... you didn't get a Red card!"

"Would you believe... that when the apple ripens, it turns into a soccer ball?"

When it comes to money, there are two types: those who make it happen and those who wonder what happened.

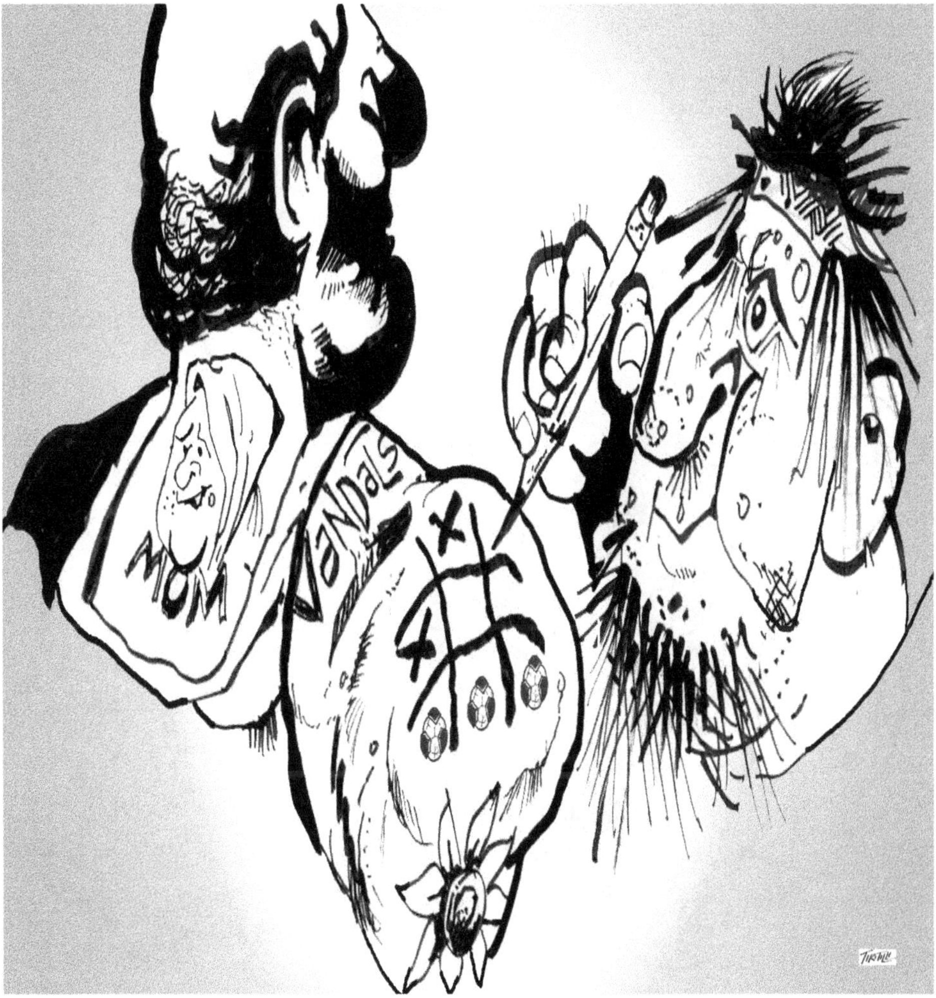
MOM
VANDALS

Tic-Tac-Toe

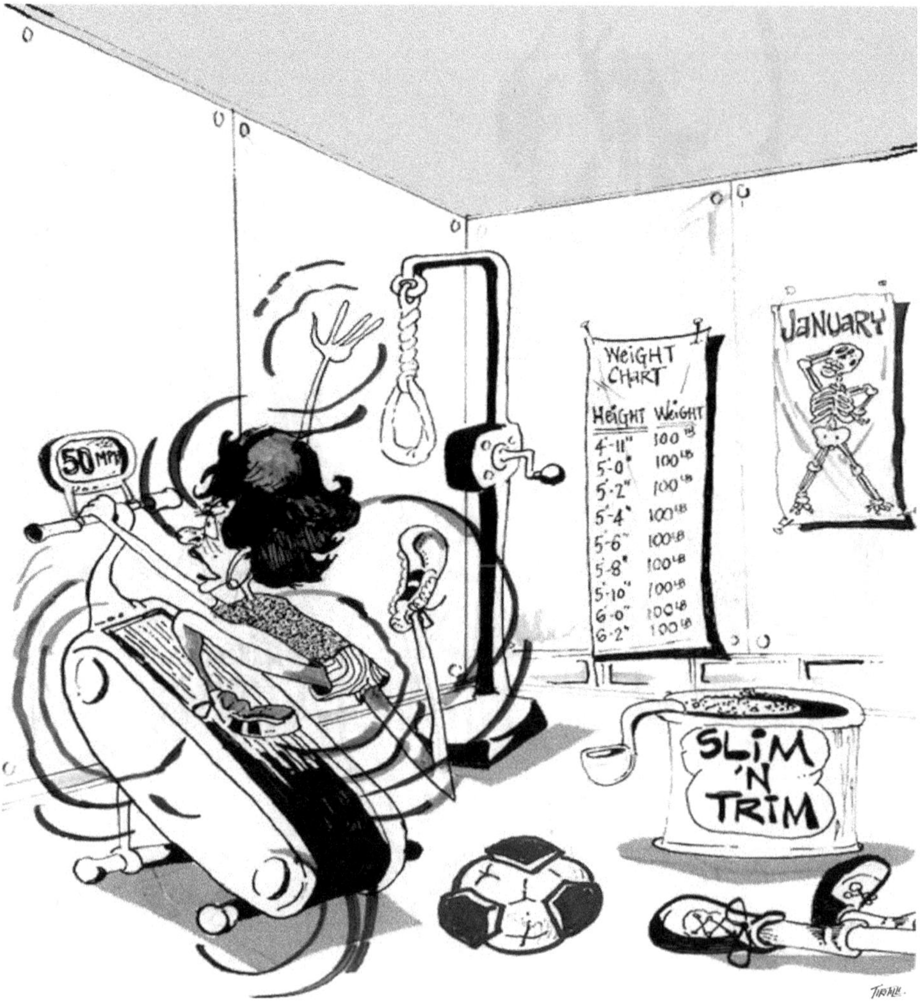

50 MPH
WEIGHT CHART
HEIGHT WEIGHT
4'-11" 100 LB
5'-0" 100 LB
5'-2" 100 LB
5'-4" 100 LB
5'-6" 100 LB
5'-8" 100 LB
5'-10" 100 LB
6'-0" 100 LB
6'-2" 100 LB
JANUARY
SLIM 'N TRIM

Soccer basic training

"Ha... your soccer future is full of PENALTIES!"

"Ha... your soccer future is full of Red Cards!"

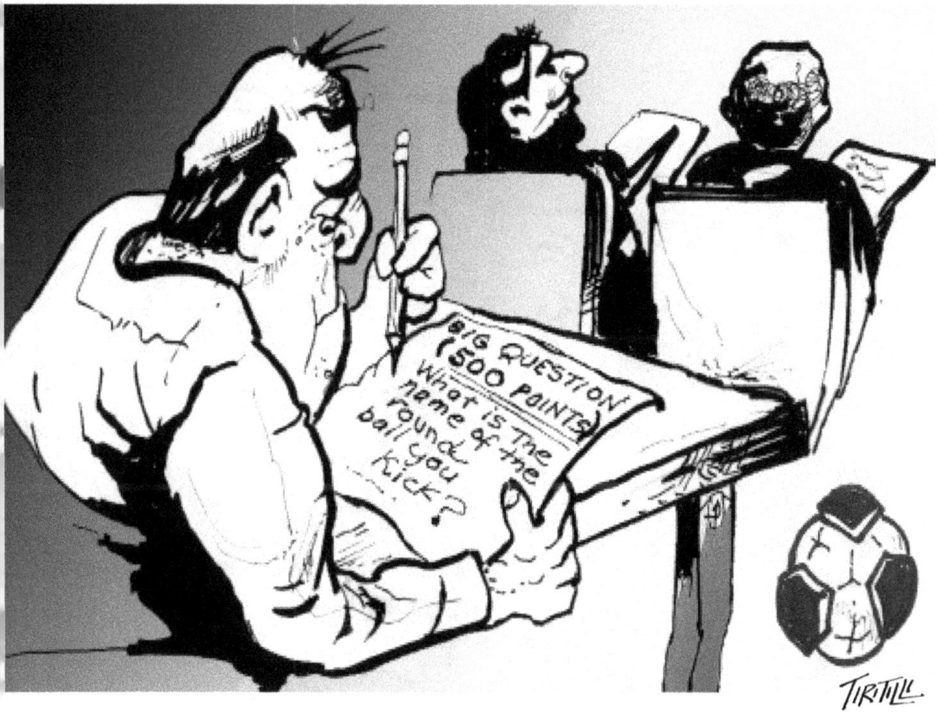
BIG QUESTION
(500 POINTS)
What is the name of the round ball you kick?

"Mirror, mirror on the wall... am I the best soccer player in the land?"

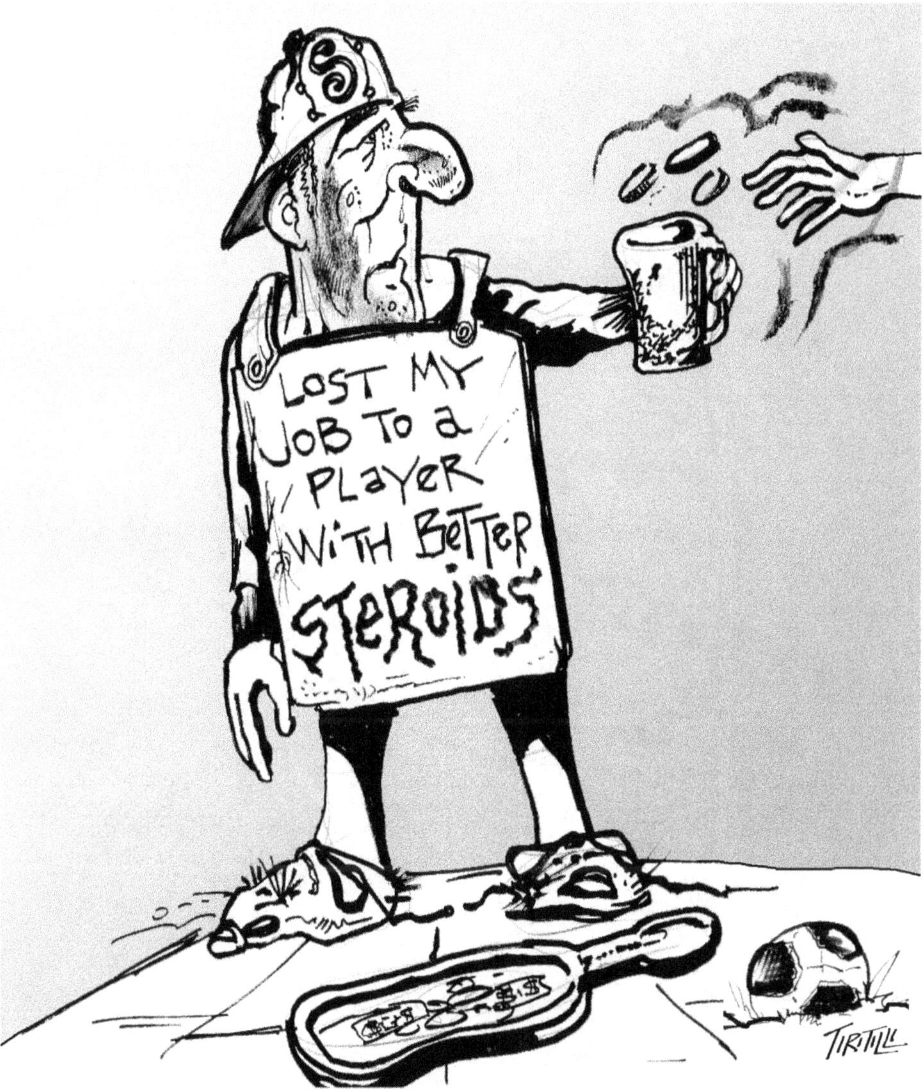
LOST MY
JOB TO a
PLAYER
WITH BETTER
STEROIDS
TIRITILLI

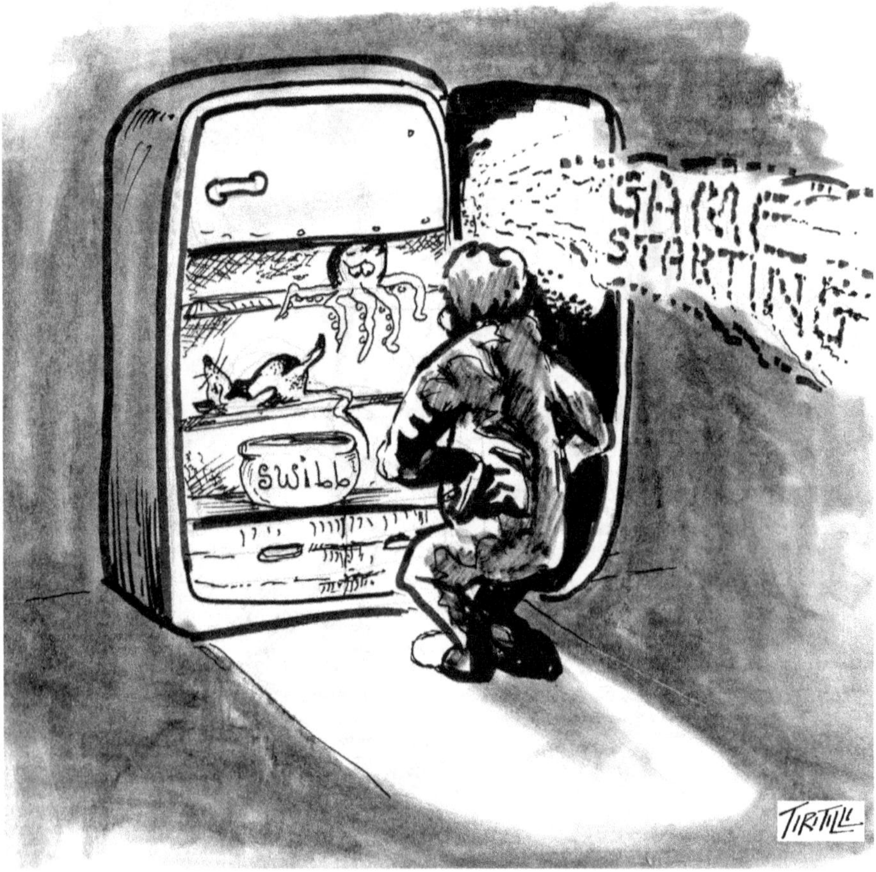
GAME
STARTING
SWILL

Nothing good to eat!

"Ha... HA... my team beat your team!"

"Who here has played in the World Cup?"

Header

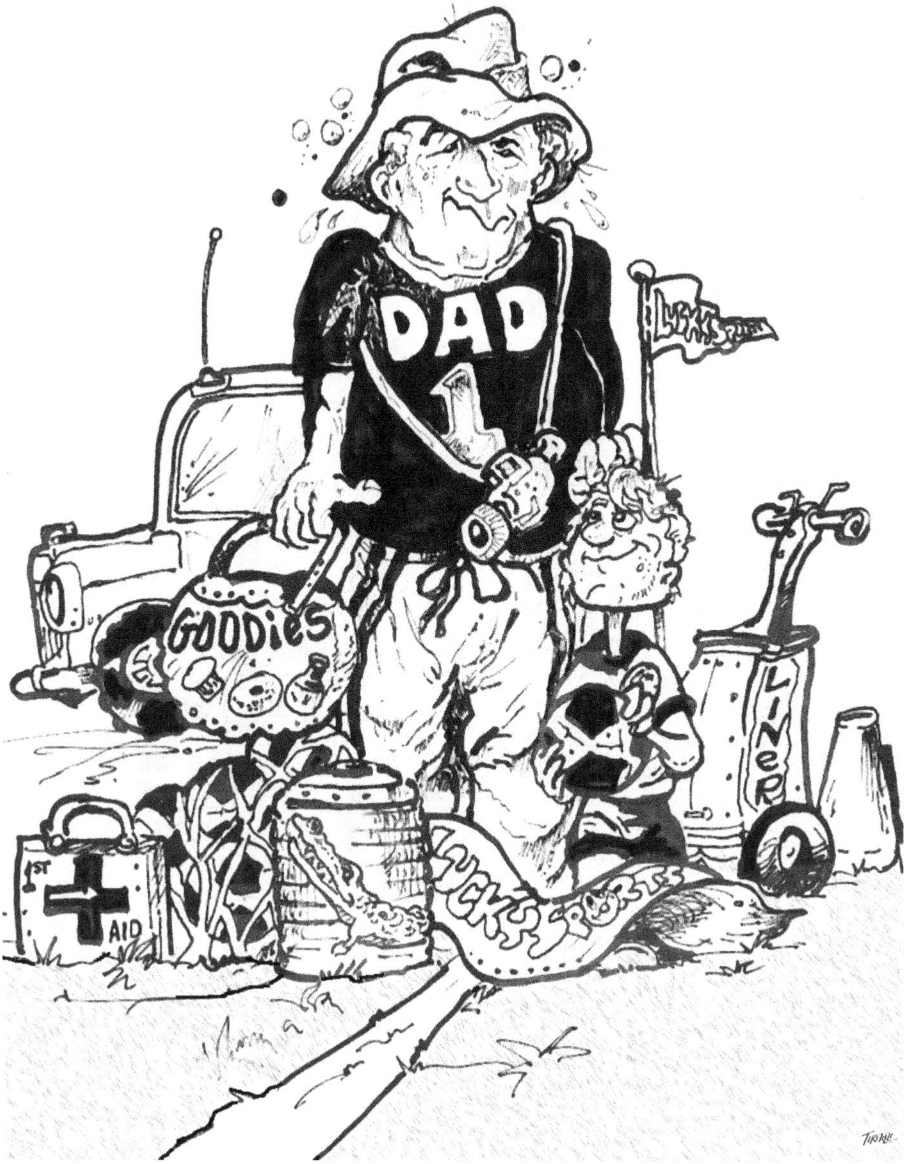
DAD
1
GOODIES
1ST
AID
LINER

Soccer Dad

Footsie falls for the FAKE!

Strike-Her

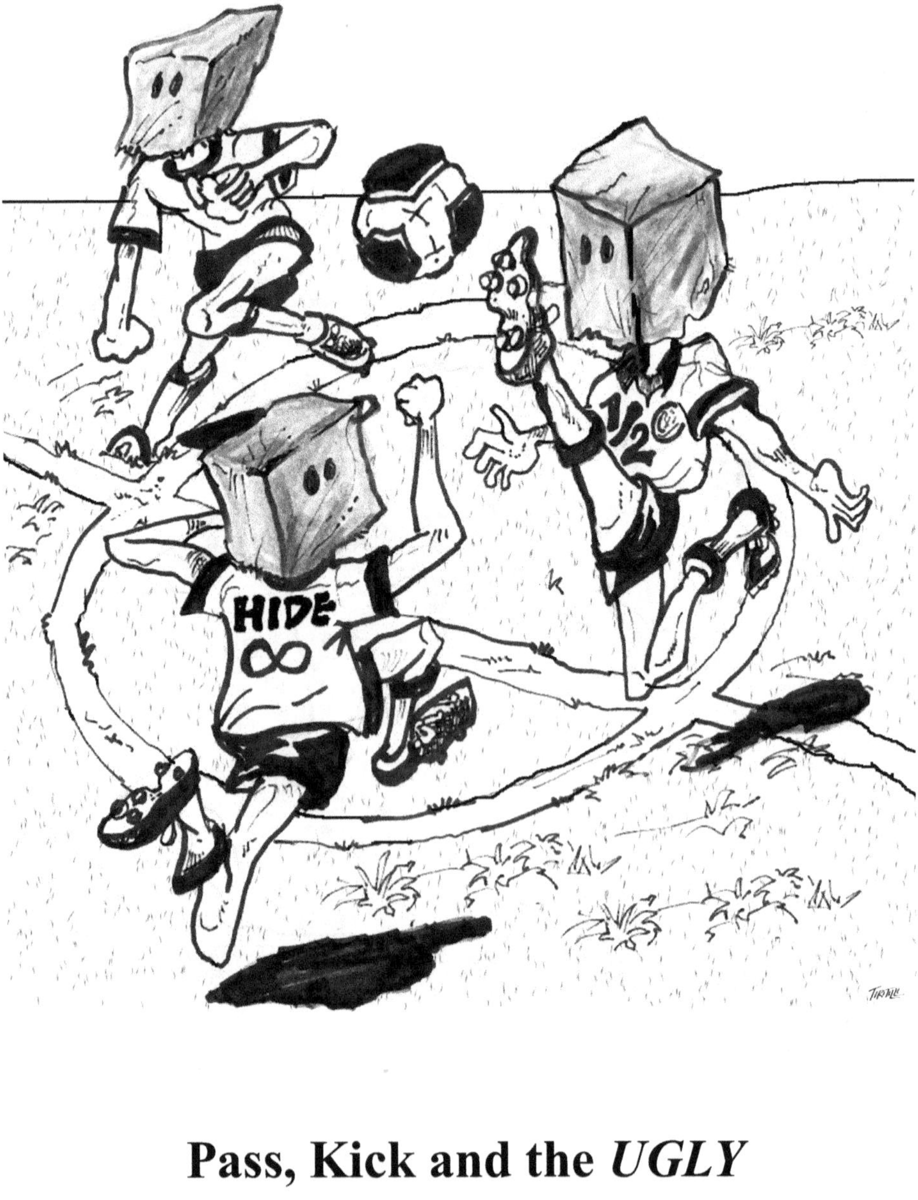
HIDE
∞
1/2

Pass, Kick and the *UGLY*

"Alright! You can wear MATCHING sweat bands!"

Lineman

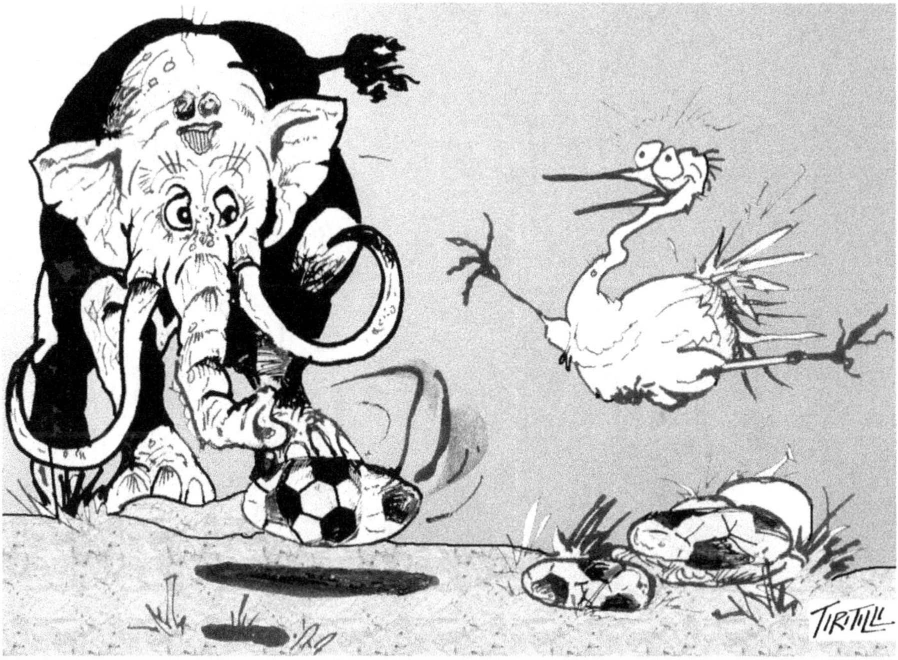
TIRITILLI

Evolution of Soccer

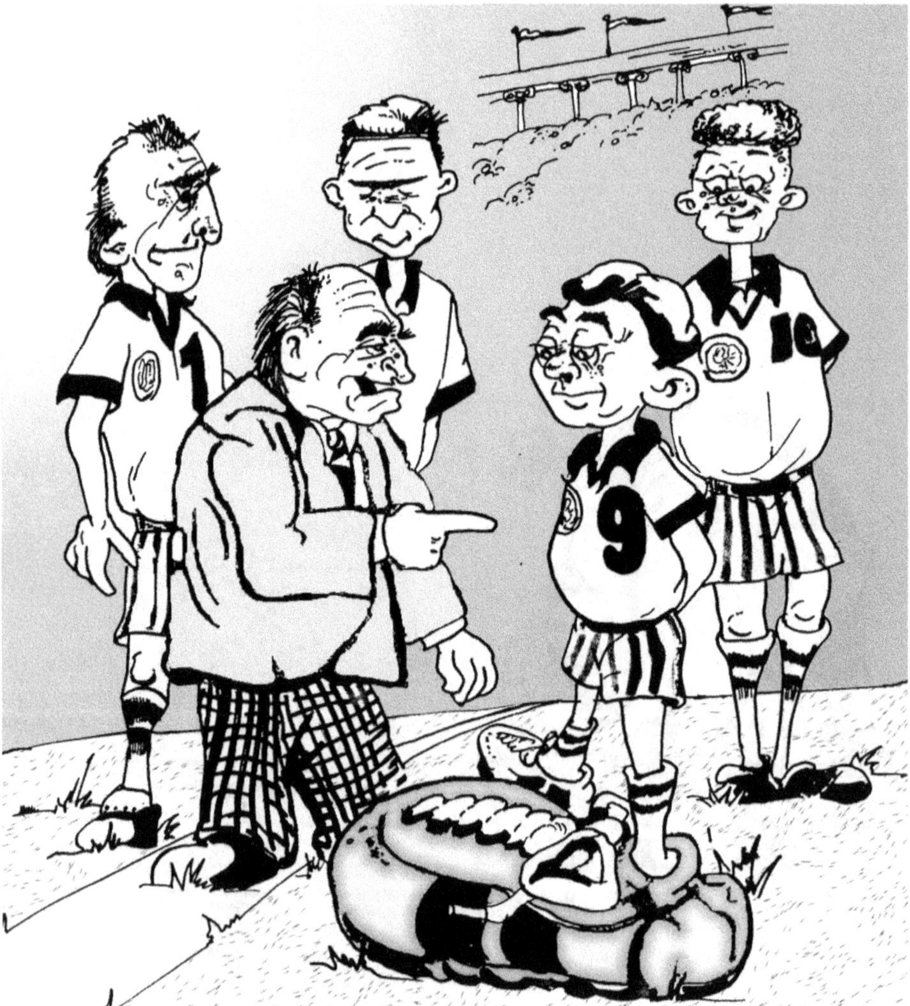
1
9
10

"So, you're BIG FOOT, huh?"

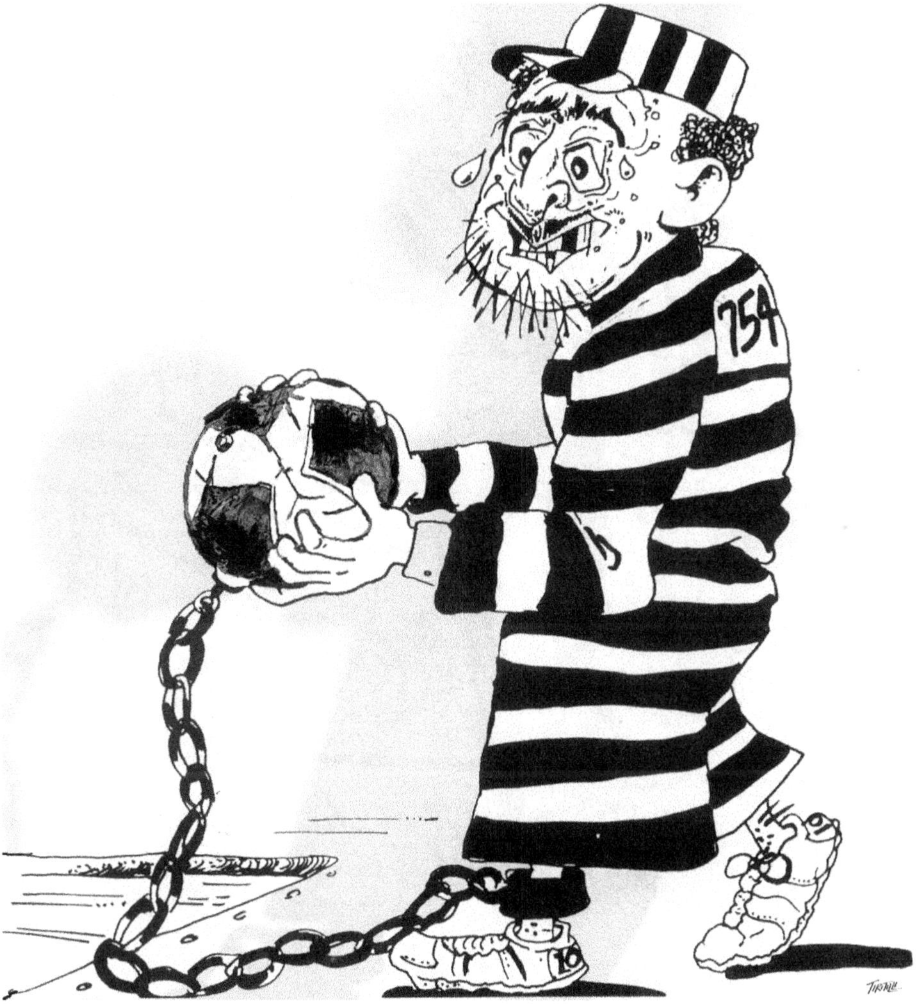
754

Too many "RED" cards

"Next time... wear separate jerseys!"

Freddie *"freezes"* at the exact moment of the final "KICKOFF".

**"You're not fat...
you're just a victim of circumference!"**

"That's my first Agony of de Feet!"

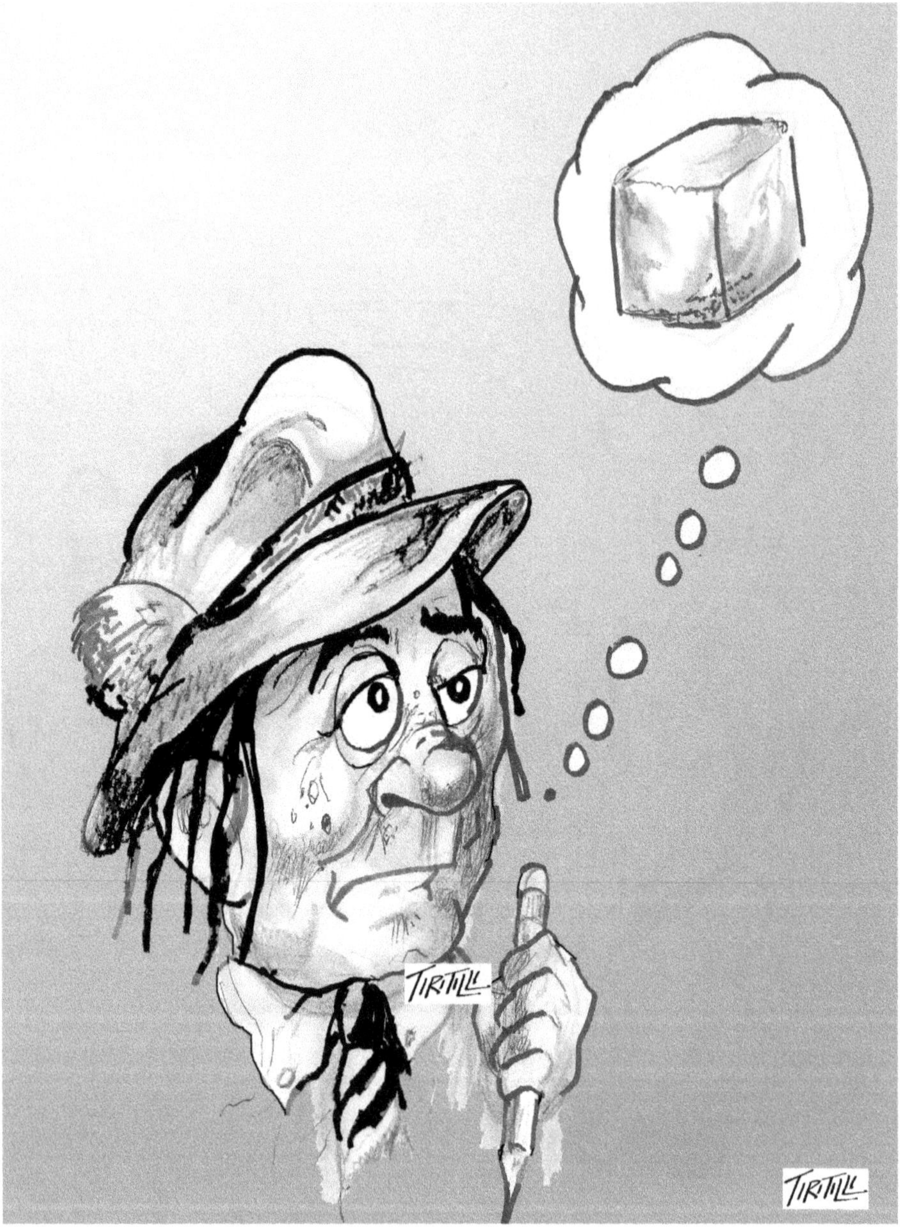
TIRITILLI
TIRITILLI

Sports writer Damon achieves writer's block

"Soccer news is NOT FAKE news!"

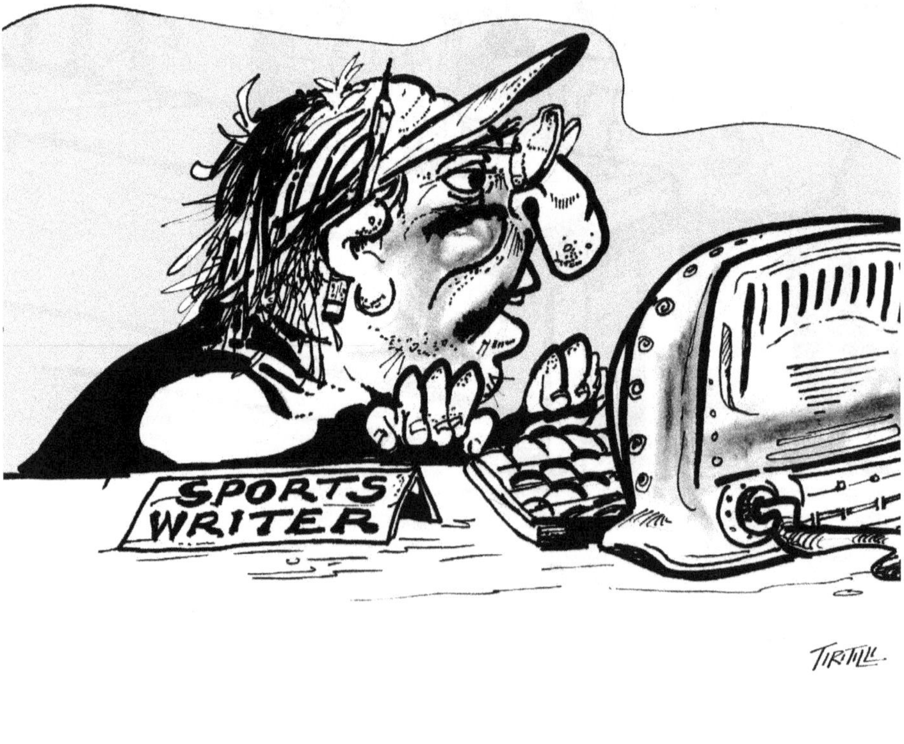
SPORTS
WRITER
TIRITILLI

"I don't write FAKE NEWS!"

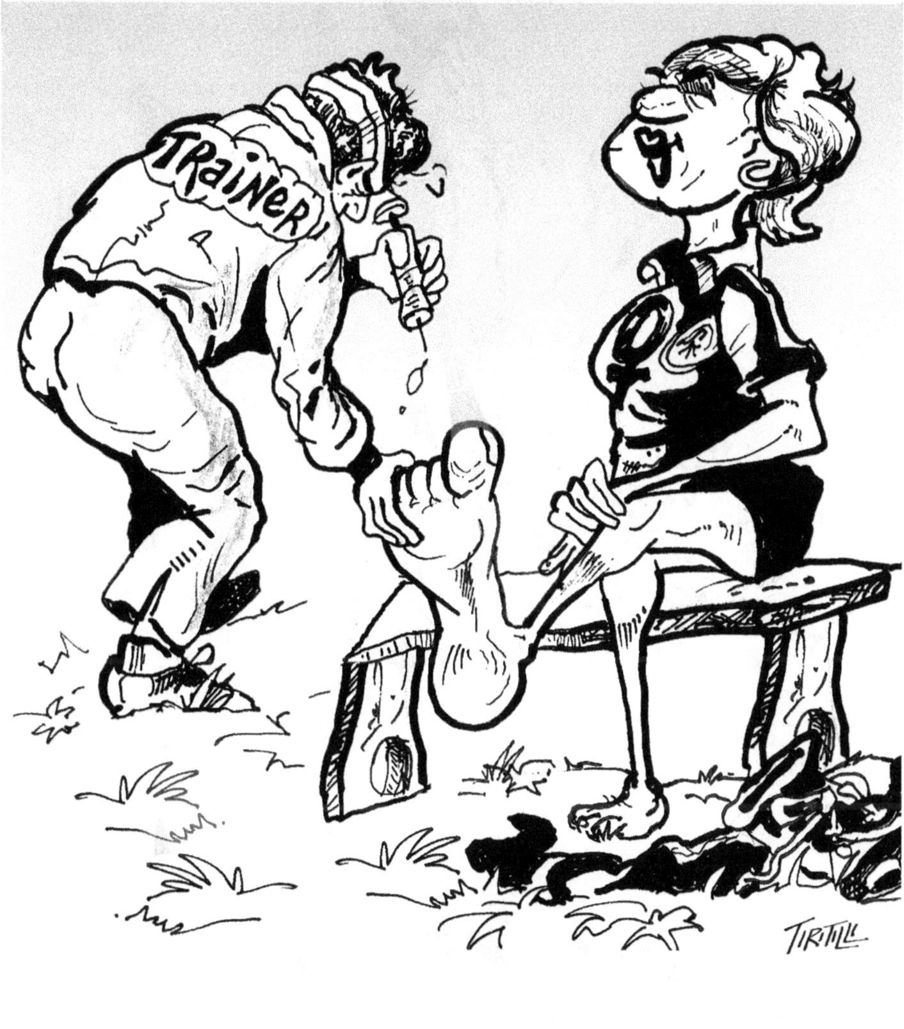
TRAINER
TIRITILLI

"I hope that's a B-12 shot!"

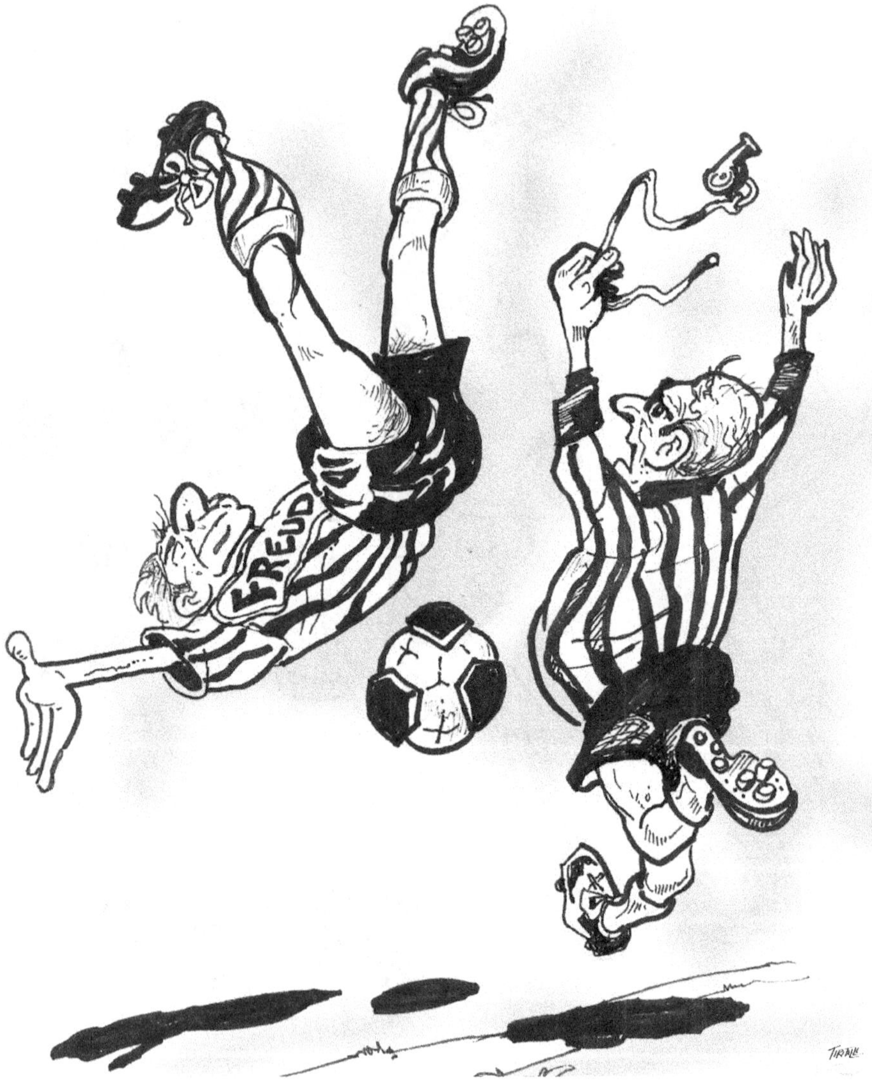
FREUD

Whoops! A Freudian slip!

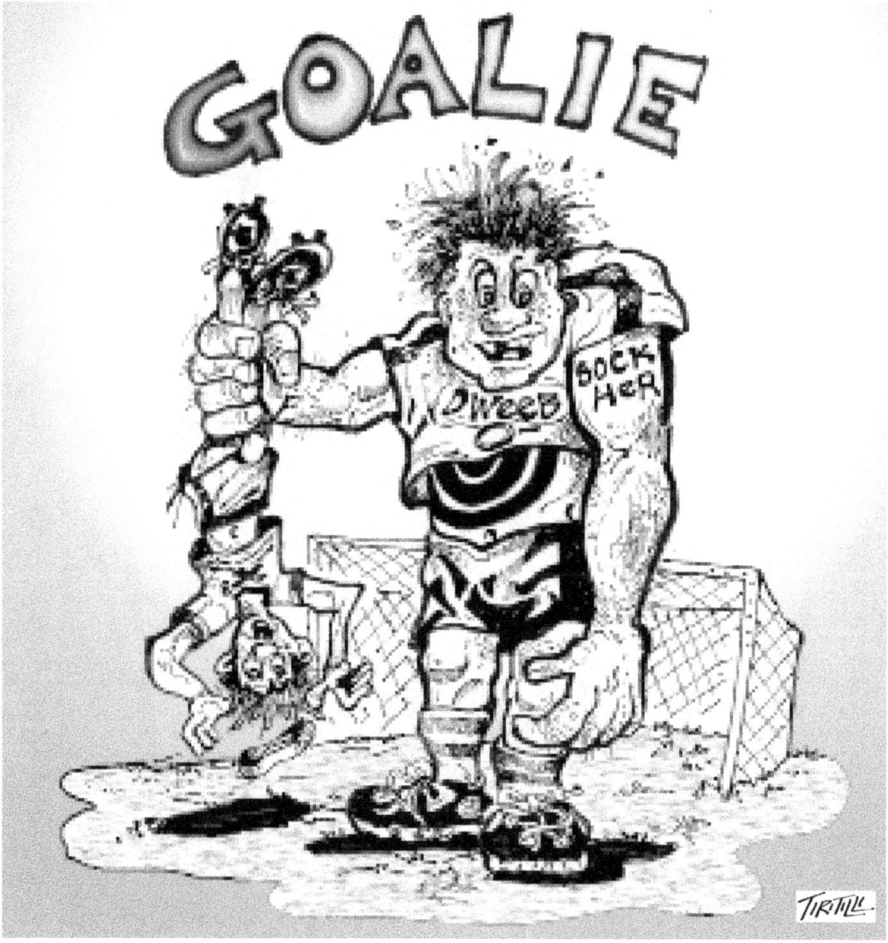
GOALIE
DWEEB
SOCK HER

Former Sumo wrestler, Sushi reaches goal of being bigger than the net.

"This is more serious than life & death...
It's about winning soccer!"

"ROCK- IT" scientists invent Soccerbot!

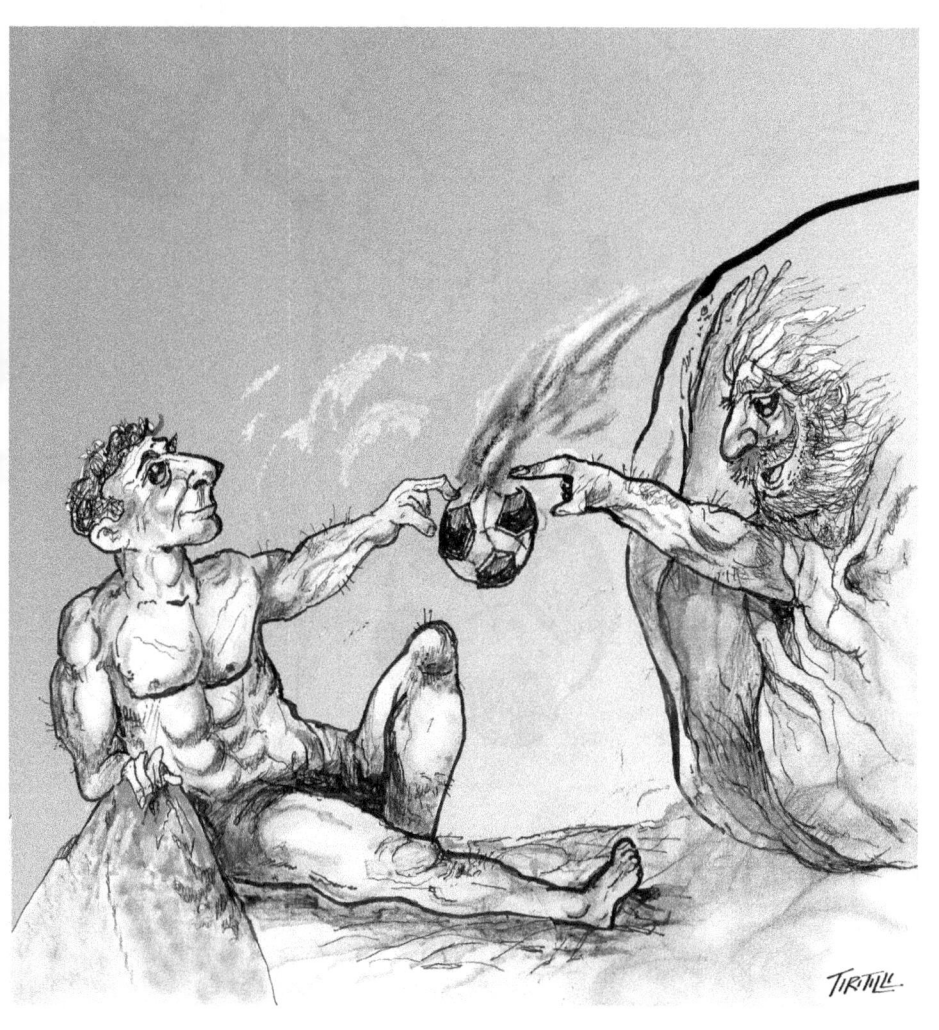

Michaelangelo creates "GOD"... GOD creates SOCCER!

Queen Mother celebrates her 200th birthday... joins Liverpool Team

"I dub thee... *Sir Loin*... well done!"

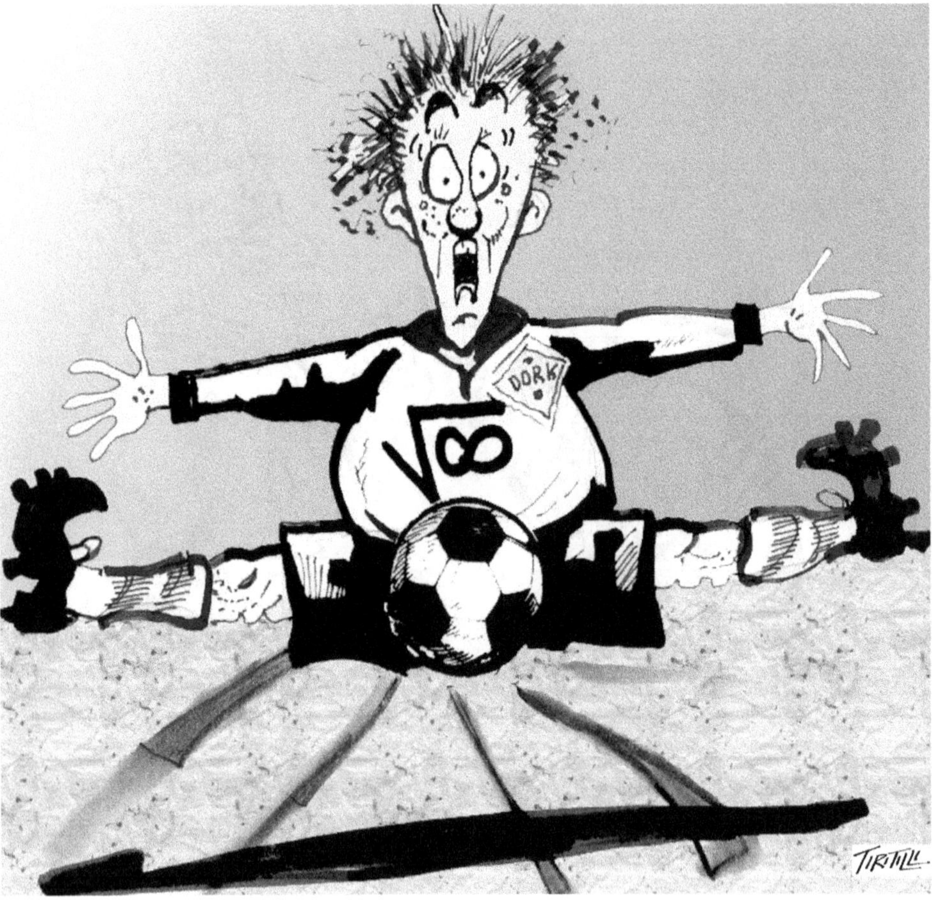
DORK

Bullseye!

**Enough of this...
that's using your head.**

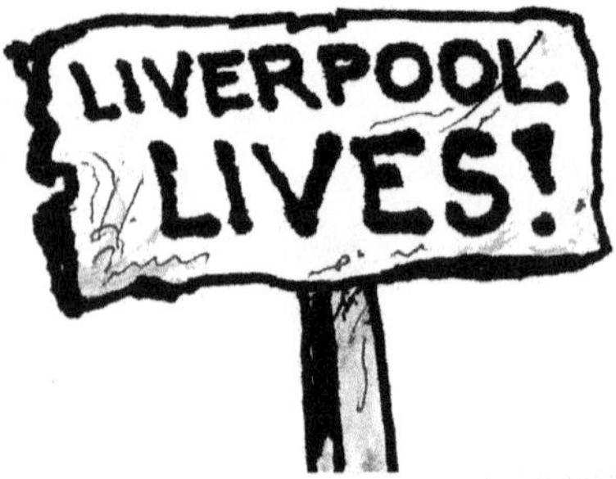
LIVERPOOL
LIVES!

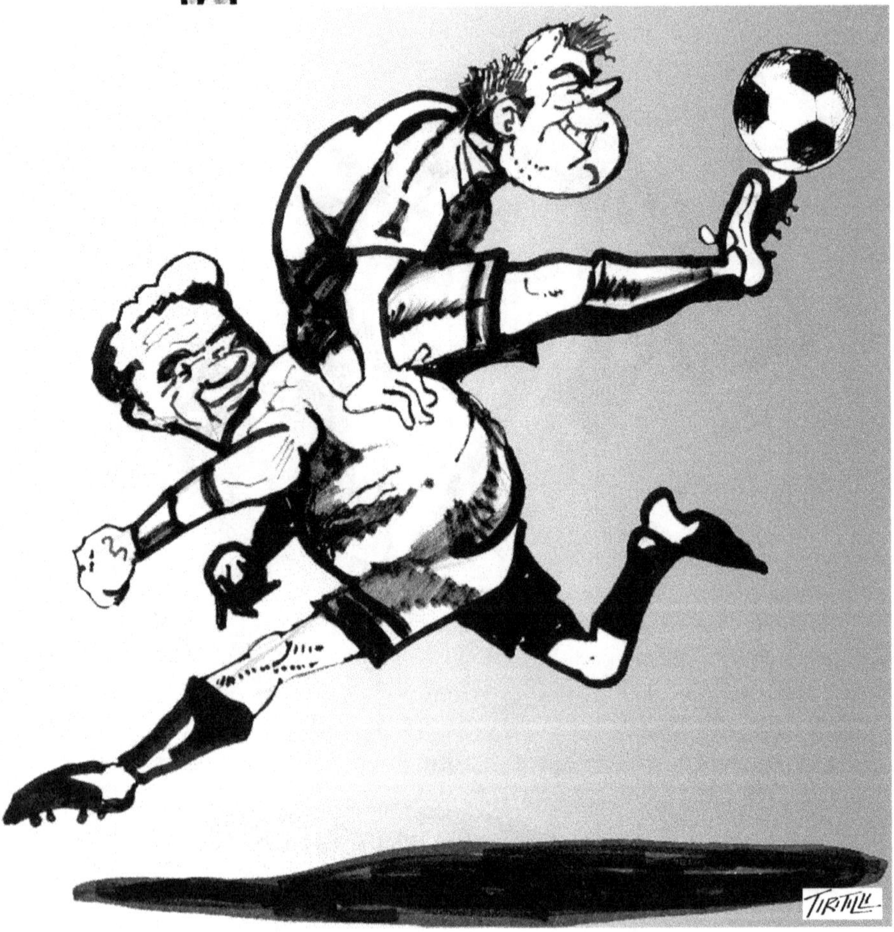

He's taking this dual striker thing a little too far.

**You can't tie up a soccer player
for very long until they free themselves.**

"Which is the soccer flag?"

Soccer player trying to kick out of a rut.

The old timer needs Geritol

Soccer's BIG GUN

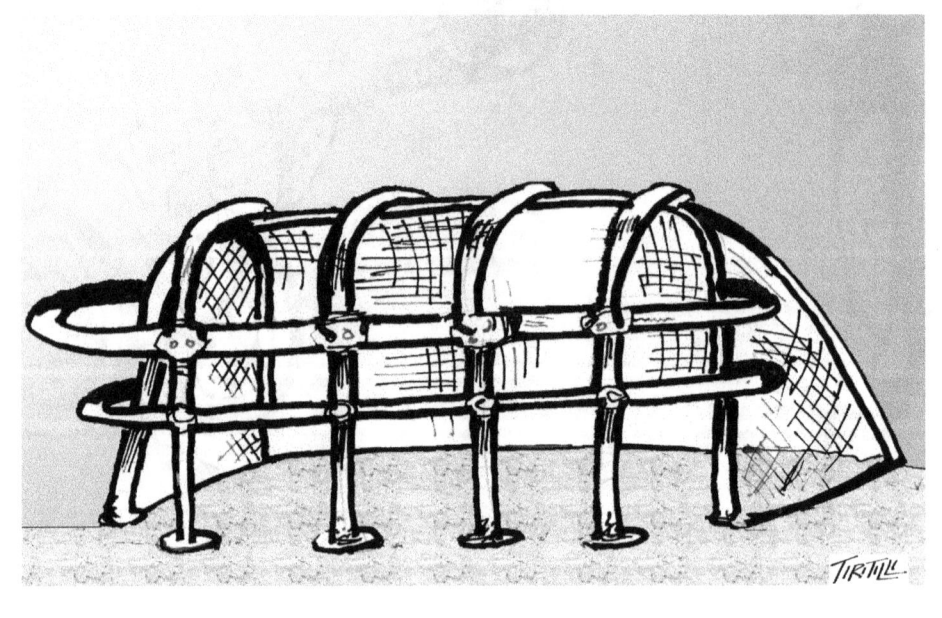

Ultimate Goalie

Water hazards

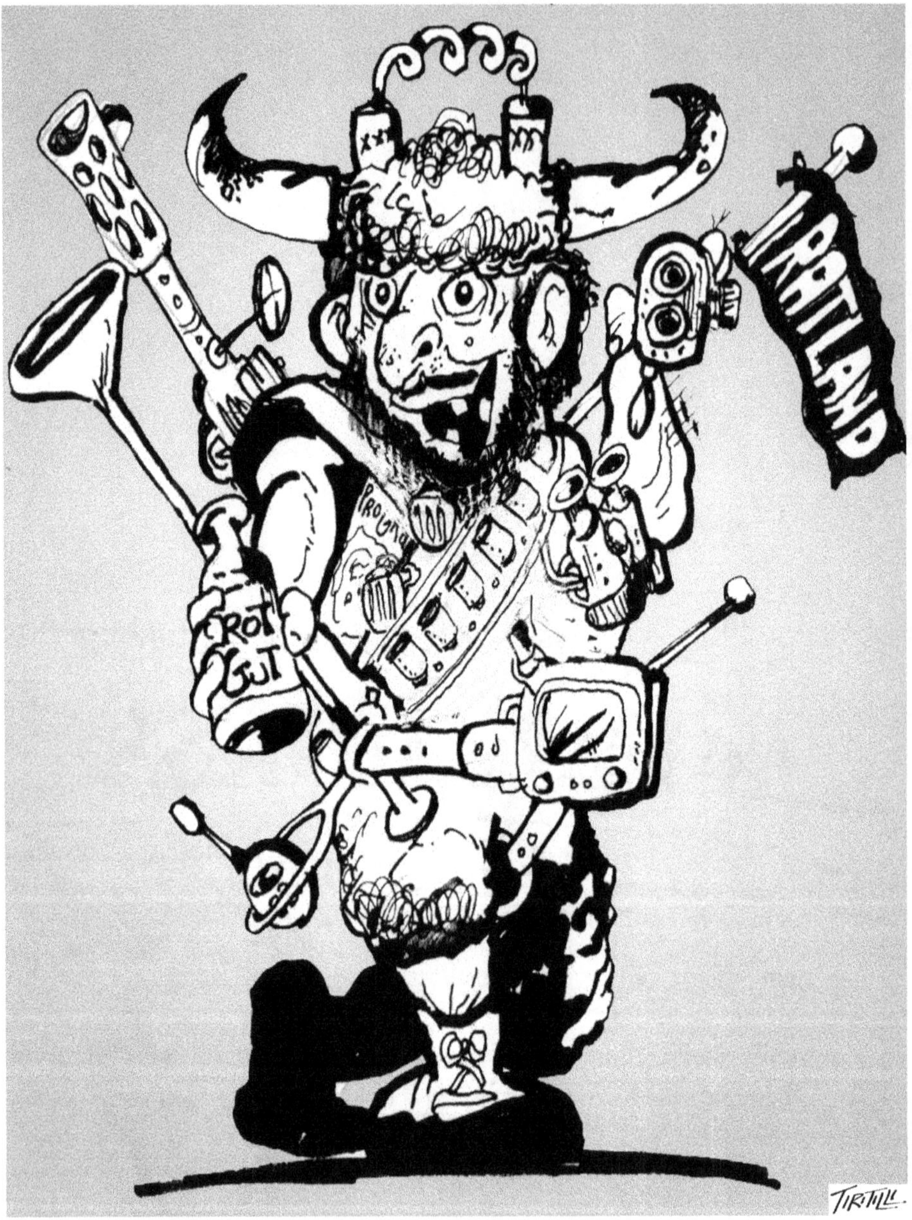
ROT GUT
TIRITILLI.

Ready for anything

"We got some time, let's practice some free kicks."

"He's our ball buster."

"Make that soccer wall taller than the one in Mexico."

New soccer ball energy drink

"My butterfly net has saved many goals from scoring."

Soccer player buried with his cleats on.

"Are you sure this stuff works?"

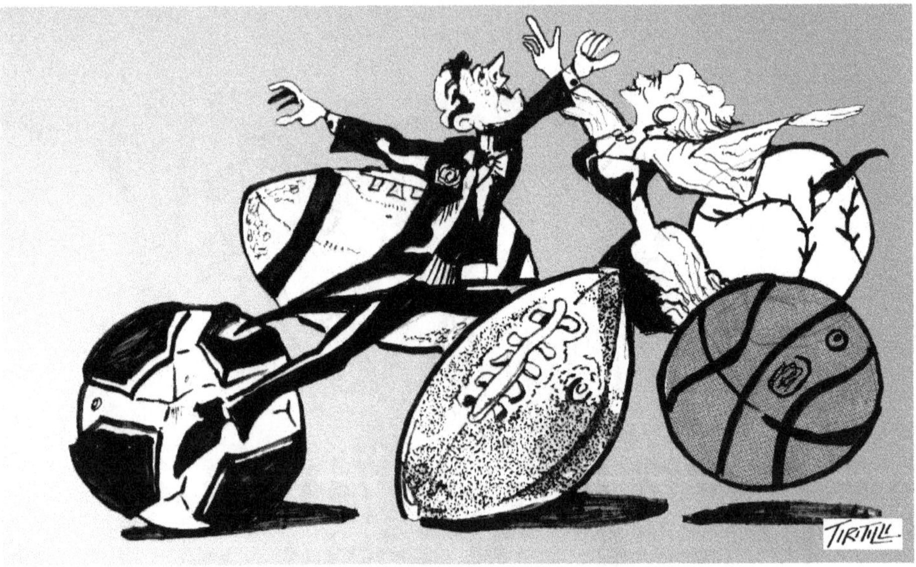
TIRITILLI

The Sports Ball

"I won betting on Liverpool."

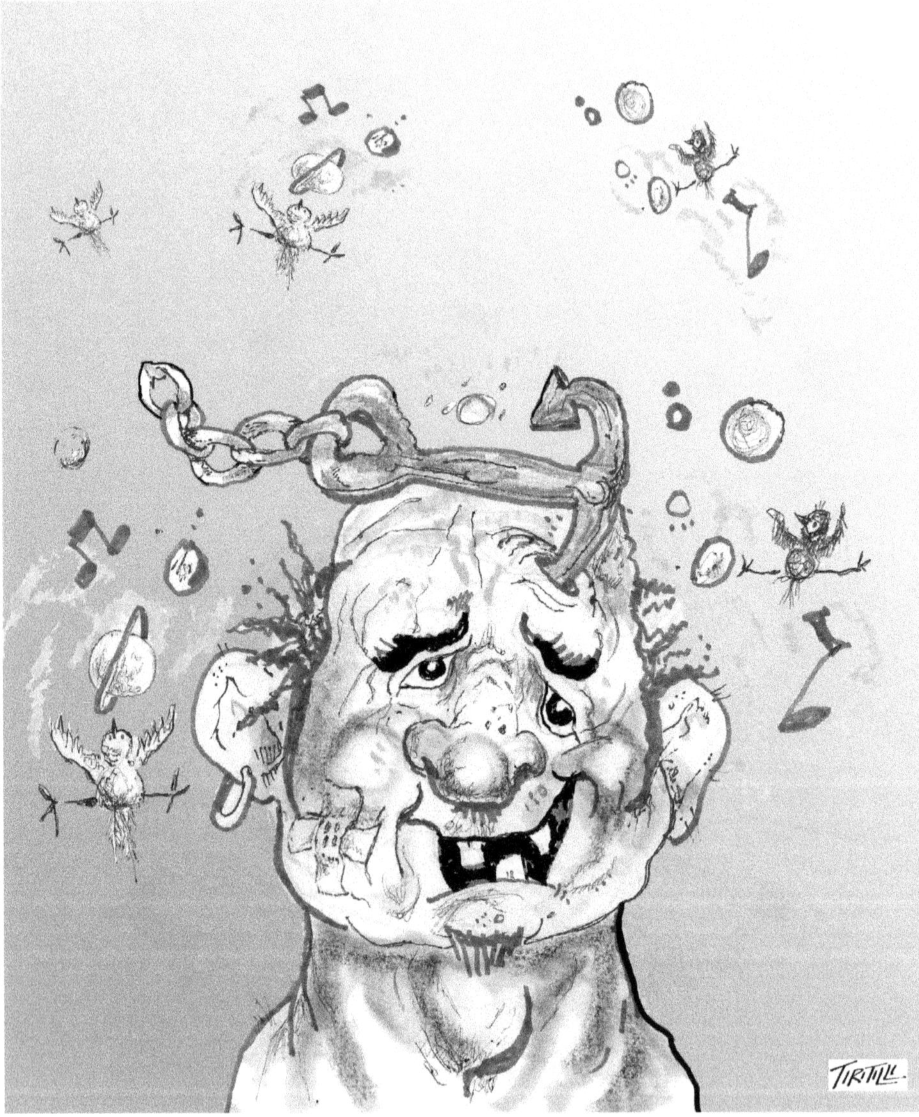
TIRITILLI.

Soccer's new posterboy!

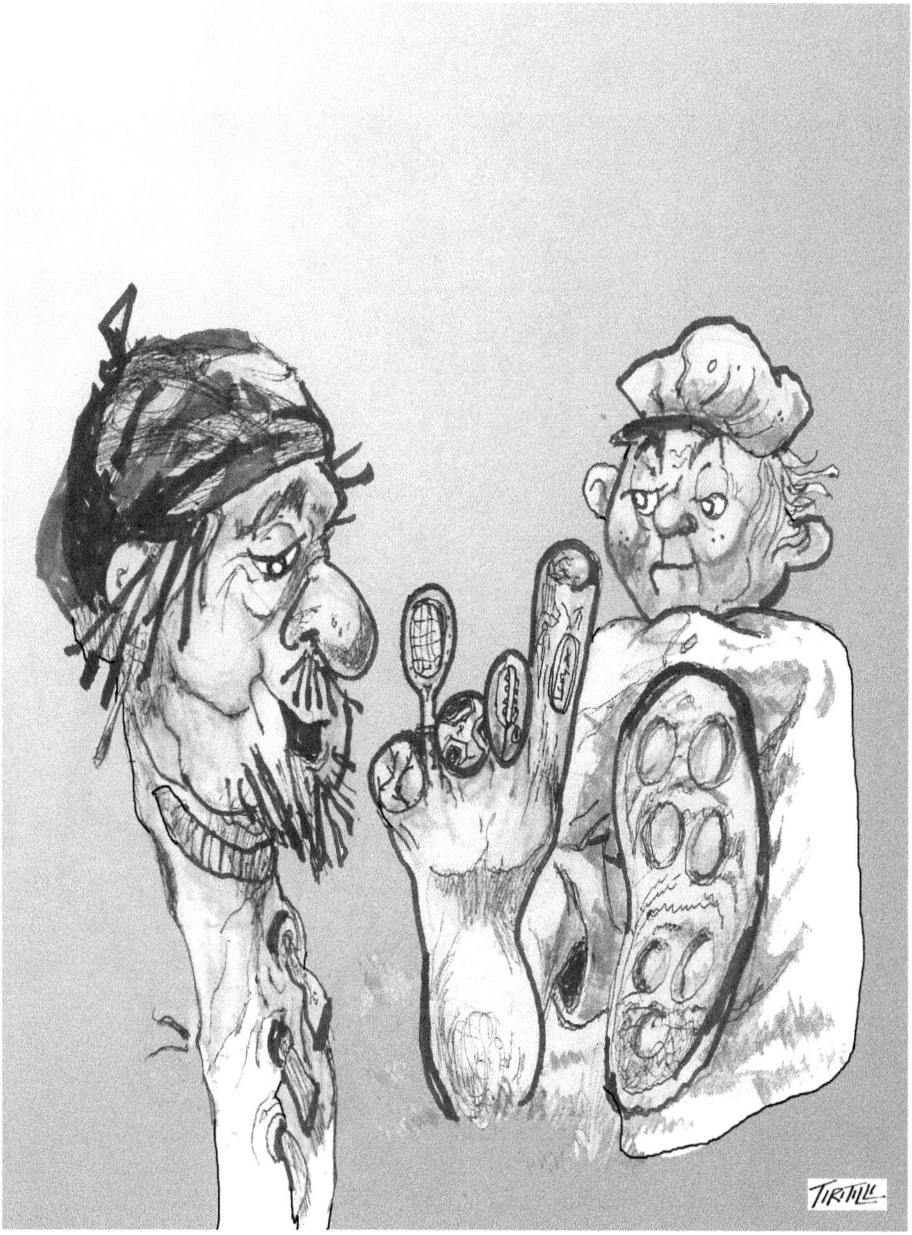
TIRITILLI

Athlete's foot

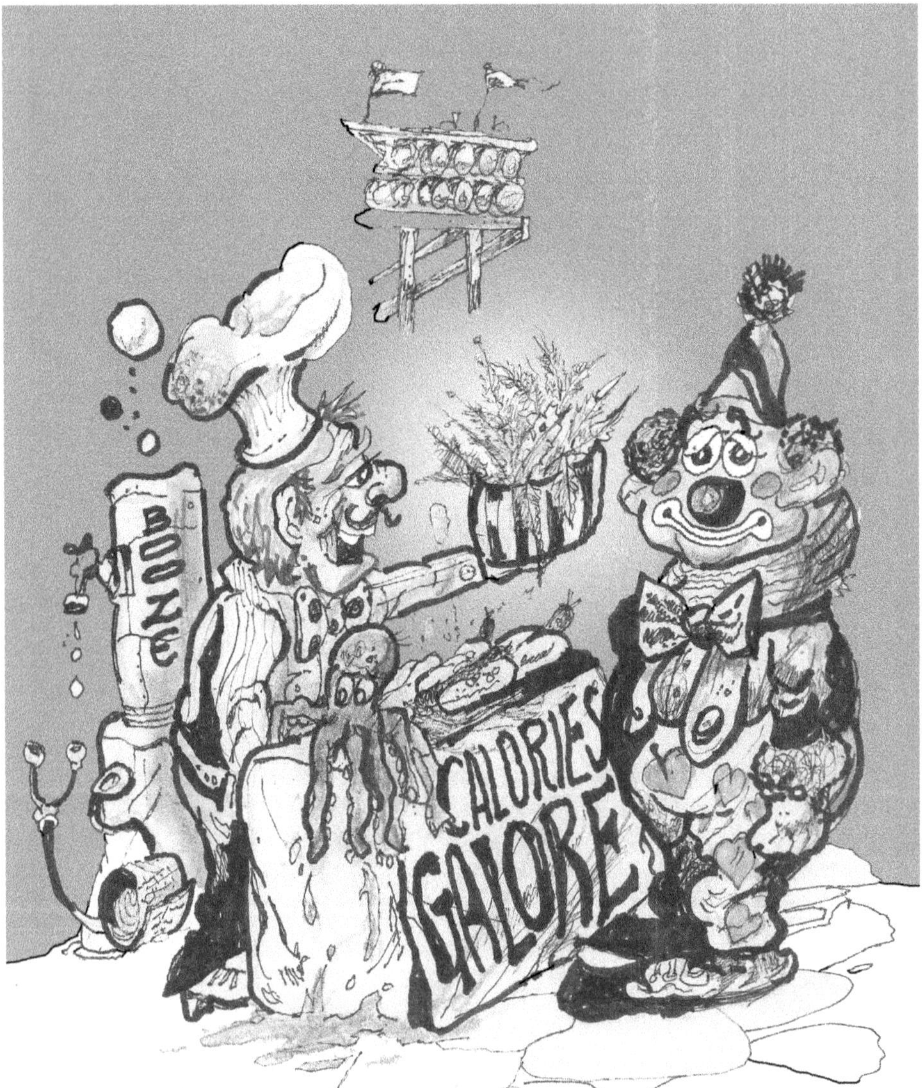
BOOZE
CALORIES
GALORE
TIRITILLI

"Feathers! Try one."

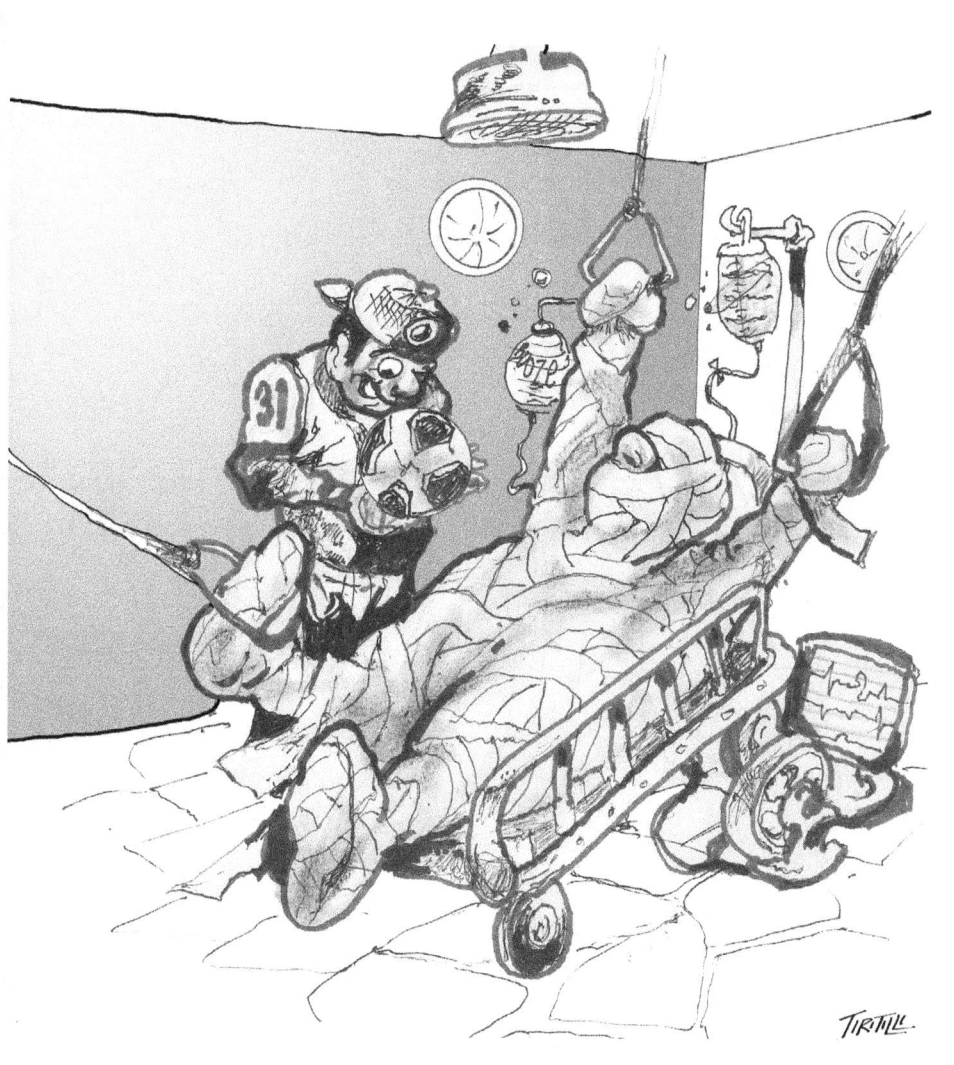

"Congratulations! They awarded you the game ball!"

"No! It's normal for goalies to *hate* you!"

"He's so slow, it takes him 90 minutes to watch 60 Minutes!"

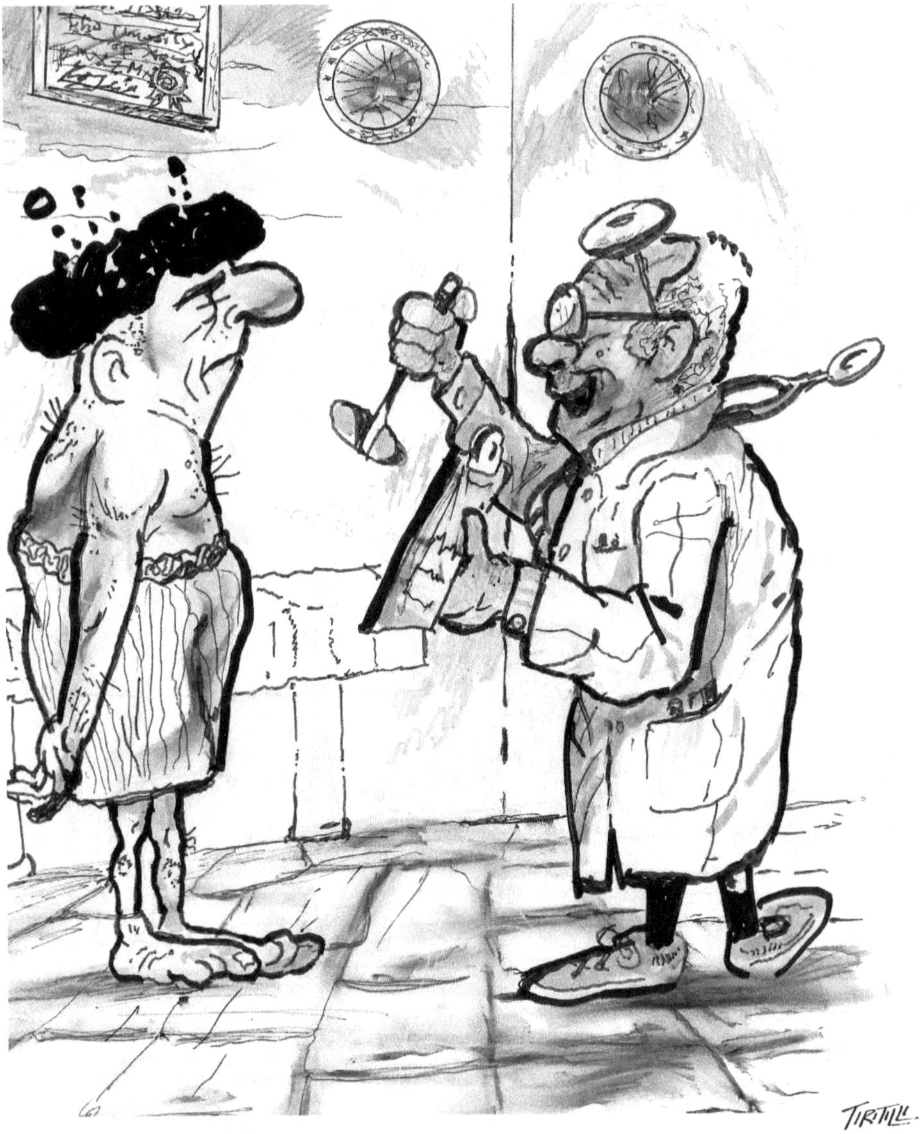
TIRITILLI.

"I recommend the World Cup to all my patients since delusions give you an excellent cardio workout!"

"Don't be sad... the game is over.
Be happy it happened!"

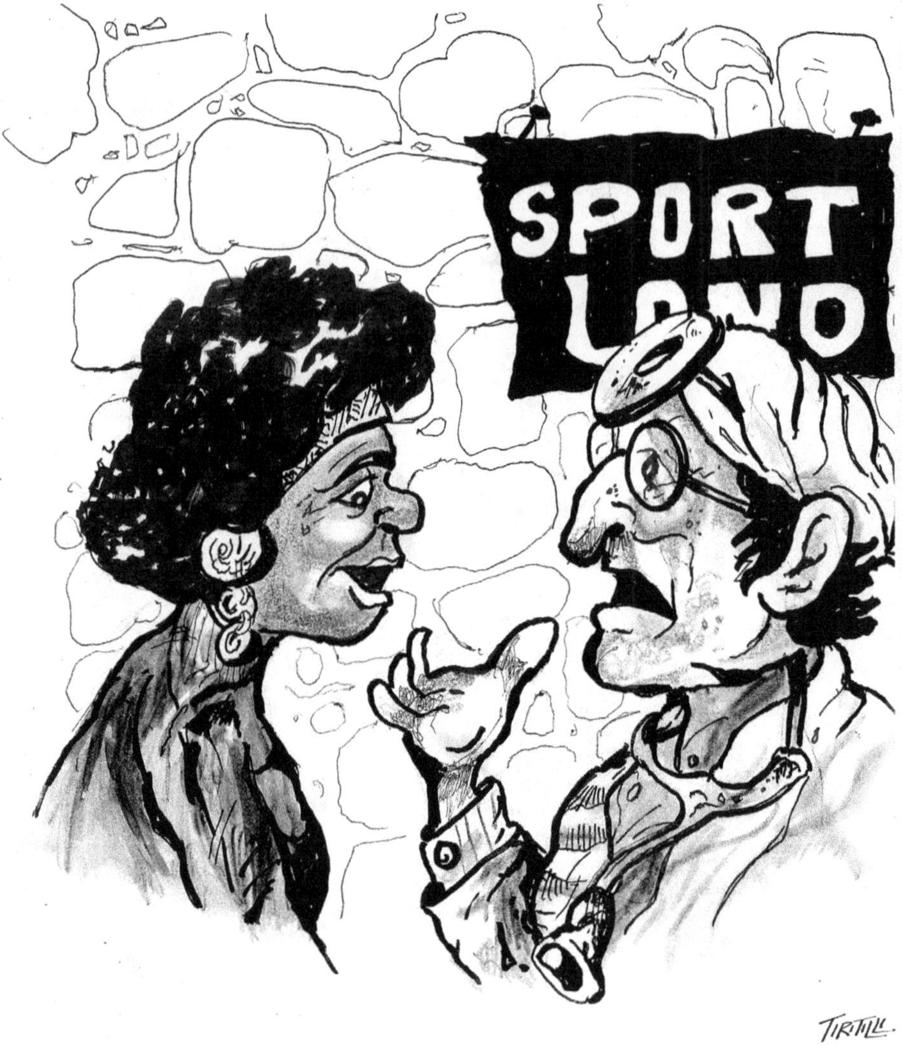
SPORT
TIRITILLI.

"I won't give you something to stop your *sleepwalking* because you need the exercise!"

"Soccer's world attitude toward sport drugs!"

"Everyone's favorite sport... buying sports equipment and goods!"

Robert A. Tiritilli

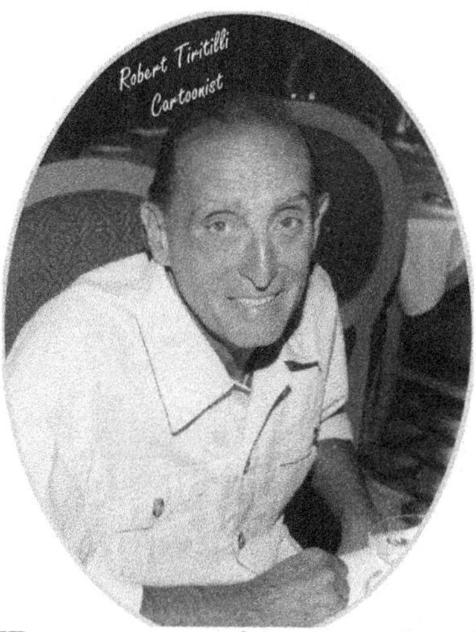
Robert Tiritilli
Cartoonist

Award-winning cartoonist, Robert A. Tiritilli—a true sports aficionado—is passionate about all sports and loves to make fun of the pastime and all those who play it. He has drawn 1,000's of different sports cartoons and creates his outlandish style of sports cartooning by combining representative portraiture with cartoonish lightheartedness.

He uses a unique sense of silliness to strike a chord with anyone who plays or enjoys sports, whether they are athletes or couch potatoes.

He finds more ways to blend humorous cartoons with crafty captions. This cartoonist plays with a deck of cards containing every shade of sports humor—wit, satire, jesting, and clowning.

Laugh until your sides hurt with his collections of hilarious sports cartoons! Tiritilli has put the "F" back into the word "FUN."

Sports has more words, terms, and phrases that lend themselves to humorous reinterpretation based on their literal meaning.

The fun of these cartoons at its best is when it shifts the meaning of a sports phrase into another one. But in some cases, the pictures take the obvious joke and make it better with a hilarious execution.

Robert A. Tiritilli

Robert A. Tiritilli is an artist who works in several mediums. His favorite is the traditional pen & ink technique, which he has produced thousands of detailed artworks. Recently, he has created several works of graphic fine art in the labor-intensive and time-consuming medium of scratchboarding. Scratchboarding is a drawing technique whereby you scratch or carve a design on the surface of a black board, revealing white underneath. It has the opposite effect of drawing with black ink on white paper. Since it is a reverse drawing method, it requires learning special techniques to master it, which Tiritilli did.

www.ingramcontent.com/pod-product-compliance
Lightning Source LLC
Chambersburg PA
CBHW071502040426
42444CB00008B/1463